THE STATES AND THE NATION SERIES, of which this volume is a part, is designed to assist the American people in a serious look at the ideals they have espoused and the experiences they have undergone in the history of the nation. The content of every volume represents the scholarship, experience, and opinions of its author. The costs of writing and editing were met mainly by grants from the National Endowment for the Humanities, a federal agency. The project was administered by the American Association for State and Local History, a nonprofit learned society, working with an Editorial Board of distinguished editors, authors, and historians, whose names are listed below.

Maryland

A Bicentennial History

Carl Bode

W. W. Norton & Company, Inc.
New York

American Association for State and Local History
Nashville

Author and publishers make grateful acknowledgment for permission to quote from The
Preston Family Papers, Special Collections, University of Maryland Library.

Published and distributed by W. W. Norton & Company, Inc.
500 Fifth Avenue
New York, New York 10036

Library of Congress Cataloguing-in-Publication Data
Bode, Carl, 1911–
    Maryland.

    (The States and the Nation series)
    Bibliography: p.
    Includes index.
    1. Maryland—History.   I. Series.
    F181.B63   975.2   77–17983
    ISBN 0–393–05672–4

Printed in the United States of America
1 2 3 4 5 6 7 8 9 0

To my fellow author
Janet Bode
with love

Contents

Contents

Illustrations

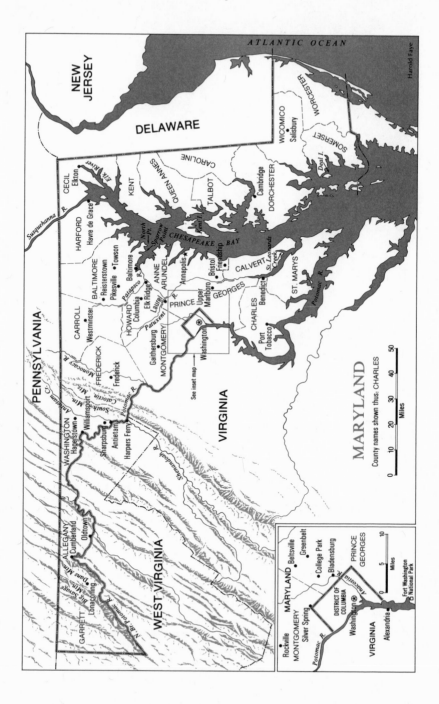

Invitation to the Reader

IN 1807, former President John Adams argued that a complete history of the American Revolution could not be written until the history of change in each state was known, because the principles of the Revolution were as various as the states that went through it. Two hundred years after the Declaration of Independence, the American nation has spread over a continent and beyond. The states have grown in number from thirteen to fifty. And democratic principles have been interpreted differently in every one of them.

We therefore invite you to consider that the history of your state may have more to do with the bicentennial review of the American Revolution than does the story of Bunker Hill or Valley Forge. The Revolution has continued as Americans extended liberty and democracy over a vast territory. John Adams was right: the states are part of that story, and the story is incomplete without an account of their diversity.

The Declaration of Independence stressed life, liberty, and the pursuit of happiness; accordingly, it shattered the notion of holding new territories in the subordinate status of colonies. The Northwest Ordinance of 1787 set forth a procedure for new states to enter the Union on an equal footing with the old. The Federal Constitution shortly confirmed this novel means of building a nation out of equal states. The step-by-step process through which territories have achieved self-government and national representation is among the most important of the Founding Fathers' legacies.

The method of state-making reconciled the ancient conflict between liberty and empire, resulting in what Thomas Jefferson called an empire for liberty. The system has worked and remains unaltered, despite enormous changes that have taken place in the nation. The country's extent and variety now surpass anything the patriots of '76 could likely have imagined. The United States has changed from an agrarian republic into a highly industrial and urban democracy, from a fledgling nation into a major world power. As Oliver Wendell Holmes remarked in 1920, the creators of the nation could not have seen completely how it and its constitution and its states would develop. Any meaningful review in the bicentennial era must consider what the country has become, as well as what it was.

The new nation of equal states took as its motto *E Pluribus Unum*—"out of many, one." But just as many peoples have become Americans without complete loss of ethnic and cultural identities, so have the states retained differences of character. Some have been superficial, expressed in stereotyped images— big, boastful Texas, "sophisticated" New York, "hillbilly" Arkansas. Other differences have been more real, sometimes instructively, sometimes amusingly; democracy has embraced Huey Long's Louisiana, bilingual New Mexico, unicameral Nebraska, and a Texas that once taxed fortunetellers and spawned politicians called "Woodpecker Republicans" and "Skunk Democrats." Some differences have been profound, as when South Carolina secessionists led other states out of the Union in opposition to abolitionists in Massachusetts and Ohio. The result was a bitter Civil War.

The Revolution's first shots may have sounded in Lexington and Concord; but fights over what democracy should mean and who should have independence have erupted from Pennsylvania's Gettysburg to the "Bleeding Kansas" of John Brown, from the Alamo in Texas to the Indian battles at Montana's Little Bighorn. Utah Mormons have known the strain of isolation; Hawaiians at Pearl Harbor, the terror of attack; Georgians during Sherman's march, the sadness of defeat and devastation. Each state's experience differs instructively; each adds understanding to the whole.

The purpose of this series of books is to make that kind of understanding accessible, in a way that will last in value far beyond the bicentennial fireworks. The series offers a volume on every state, plus the District of Columbia—fifty-one, in all.

Each book contains, besides the text, a view of the state through eyes other than the author's—a "photographer's essay," in which a skilled photographer presents his own personal perceptions of the state's contemporary flavor.

We have asked authors not for comprehensive chronicles, nor for research monographs or new data for scholars. Bibliographies and footnotes are minimal. We have asked each author for a summing up—interpretive, sensitive, thoughtful, individual, even personal—of what seems significant about his or her state's history. What distinguishes it? What has mattered about it, to its own people and to the rest of the nation? What has it come to now?

To interpret the states in all their variety, we have sought a variety of backgrounds in authors themselves and have encouraged variety in the approaches they take. They have in common only these things: historical knowledge, writing skill, and strong personal feelings about a particular state. Each has wide latitude for the use of the short space. And if each succeeds, it will be by offering you, in your capacity as a *citizen* of a state *and* of a nation, stimulating insights to test against your own.

James Morton Smith
General Editor

ACKNOWLEDGMENTS

Much of my indebtedness in the making of this book involves the College Park campus of the University of Maryland, where I teach. I'm grateful to the English Department head, Shirley Kenny, and associate head, Charles Rutherford, for assigning Michele Bissonette as my research assistant, and especially grateful to Michele herself. I'm grateful to Mary Boccaccio of the Maryland Room in the McKeldin Library and her colleagues Nancy Walton, Laurie Sebo, and Georgia Rhodes for their frequent assistance; to Betty Baehr, the loan librarian at McKeldin, for coaxing rare books out of reluctant libraries; to Associate Dean Robert Menzer of the Graduate School for a typing grant; to Stephanie Koziski for doing the typing; and to Provost Robert Corrigan for his aid and support. Further afield I had assistance which should be acknowledged from Edith M. Bagot of the Maryland Room at the Prince Georges Community Library in Adelphi; from Marjorie Jones and Morgan Pritchett at the Enoch Pratt Library in Baltimore; and from Jo Champlin in part of the proofreading. From Nashville I got the good counsel and encouragement of Timothy Jacobson and Gerald George. And back home, finally, I got the good counsel and encouragement of Charlotte Smith Bode. It all helped.

C. B.

A Personal Word from the Author

I know the temptation to skip prefaces. But you might glance at this one because it briefly tells what the book is and isn't. It isn't a linear history of Maryland. Maryland is something like 350 years old and the books in this series are limited to 200 pages of text. If I tried to cover all those years the generalizations would be so vague that I'd sound like the *Encyclopaedia Britannica* on a gray day. What I've done instead is to write a book of episodes, roughly chronological. I've picked persons and events with an eye to ways they illuminated Maryland's past. Then I've told their story in some detail. I've wanted to make a mosaic for you, often in contrasting tones. For instance, after hearing George Alsop proclaim the attractions of colonial Maryland and seeing how Daniel Dulany benefited handsomely from them, you're introduced to Ebenezer Cooke, who jeers at the same attractions. Or you get a picture of Eastern Shore life between two sections about life in Baltimore.

Throughout the book I've tried to give a sense of the variety as well as the quality of the Maryland experience. For the sake of both I've had to make omissions, usually small though sometimes not (but remember those 200 pages). You won't find the *Ark* and the *Dove* or Thomas Stone the Signer or even some of the wars when they didn't affect Maryland very much directly. Instead you'll find—among many other things—a good deal

about Maryland's bumptious politics, a sketch of Maryland's
Daniel Boone, named Cresap; a picture of free blacks in antebellum Maryland; the story of the *Hagerstown Almanac;* a
memoir about a born-again Shoreman and another of coal miners' life near Cumberland; and a view of what went on in a pair
of middle-class households, perhaps the ancestors of our own,
as reflected in the domestic correspondence of a Mr. and Mrs.
Preston and in the scrapbooks of the parents of H. L. Mencken.

The other thing you ought to know is that I thought it would
be more useful and interesting to write about the somewhat dis-
tant past than about the immediate one. In the twentieth century,
when we leave World War II and enter the Age of Eisenhower,
we encounter a period which many of today's readers know
from the start; so there's not much in the book about our last
three decades. However, the Maryland of the eighteenth century
and, to a smaller extent, of the nineteenth century, was almost
like another country, a bit like England in relation to America.
That's why in a book as brief as this it's a good idea to spend
most of our time getting a sense of that Maryland. And that's
where my emphasis lies.

Let me add that I enjoyed writing the book—I don't belong to
the "splendid misery" school of authorship—and I trust you
enjoy reading it.

CARL BODE

Maryland

Preview

LISTEN to George Alsop, the colony's first public relations man. An artful exaggerator, he's trying to lure us from a not very merry England, across the Atlantic, and into the Brave New World. He does so in an amiably raunchy style, opening his promotional pamphlet, *A Character of the Province of Maryland* (published in London in 1666, and dedicated to the Proprietor, Cecilius Calvert, Lord Baltimore), with "Maryland is a province situated upon the large extending bowels of America." Blandly he assures us that it's the new Garden of Eden we can occupy in our "Adamitical or primitive situation." He vows that the vegetation is both lovely and useful. The wildlife is succulent; deer are so numerous that even servants sup on venison. The animals which might do harm—wolves, bears, panthers—are rare and even when they venture near the plantations they merely pounce on a pig. The sight of man "terrifies them dreadfully." Birds abound. Do we want to taste the novel delights of the turkey, "an extraordinary fat fowl, whose flesh is very pleasant and sweet"? Alsop has seen them by the hundreds.

Those settlers who've preceded us are as pleasant and sweet as the turkey. They sport a perpetual smile. Maryland's Protestants and Catholics "concur in a unanimous parallel of friendship and inseparable love." They are not only loving—they are democratic. The colony enjoys an elected assembly, which

3

meets every year for some six weeks. Its members are ordinary householders, whose good conscience helps them solve the colony's slight problems.

The colony is saved from a surfeit of democracy through the presence of two clearly defined classes, masters and servants, an arrangement authorized by God. Each class has its rights and responsibilities. Alsop has been an indentured servant himself and is eager to attract persons willing to indenture themselves to a Maryland master for a term of years. He doesn't want to seduce them or inveigle them from their English hearths. It's just that he loves his countrymen so much that he yearns to improve their lot and knows that indenture is the way to do it. Incidentally, anyone who says that servants in Maryland are abused lies in a most hellish way.

Once the male servants end their indenture they receive ample rewards, guaranteed by law. Alsop reports that these include fifty acres of land, tools to cultivate that land, corn to feed the settlers for a whole year, and three suits of clothes with accessories. The female servants, he writes with what must have been a small leer, will find the best of treatment waiting for them. Even if their virginity is tarnished, they may shorten their indenture by marrying their master. "No sooner on shore than they are courted into a copulative matrimony."

Diving into economics he reports that the main commodities are tobacco, furs, and meat. Tobacco is the prime crop for export; it pays for the many English goods, from soft silk to iron hinges, which Maryland planters require. It's also the colony's current coin. The furs, supplied by obliging Indians, include beaver, elk, and otter. The only meat for export Alsop mentions is pork.

The fur trade reminds him of the Indians so he proceeds to offer us "A Relation of the Customs, Manners, Absurdities, and Religion" of the Susquehannas. All candor, he promises to tell us only about those Indians he has seen or, as he phrases it in his lofty prose, has had an ocular experimental view of. Not surprisingly, Maryland's Indians are the noblest of them all. The men stand seven feet high; the women are dusky beauties. When the men go to war they coat their faces, arms, and chests with red, green, black, and white paint. They grease their long hair with bear's oil, bind a diadem of beads around it, and stick swan's feathers into it. They slip small hatchets beneath their belts and carry either guns or bows and arrows. Then they run out howling till they meet and, of course, vanquish their enemies. Inevitably their women are obedient and never wear the breeches.

How many restless or desperate Londoners thumbed through Alsop's pamphlet in the late 1660s and the 1670s no one knows. But we can guess that it had some effect. And also that those newcomers to Maryland weren't too disenchanted, provided they survived the ocean voyage and the initial adjustment. For if we allow for Alsop's itch to exaggerate, he made a reasonably accurate report. The colony wasn't the Garden of Eden but it wasn't the Pilgrims' stern and rockbound coast either. It wasn't a theological Utopia but it began by setting a high standard of religious toleration. The Susquehannas weren't seven feet tall but they were often noble savages and kinder to the white invader than he deserved.

1

Daniel Dulany: The Right Time, the Right Place

1. Striver in a Brown Bob Wig

WE can start with a success story, the story of one man who more than any other symbolized in his career the history of Maryland as a colony. Daniel Dulany's rise was splendid, his success clear-cut. The colony's success was both vaster and vaguer but undeniable. We'll look into both. But there's more to both than impressive achievement. Two other men, closely associated with Dulany, can illustrate two other aspects of Maryland's history. They were Tom Macnemara and Tom Cresap; each was surprisingly attractive to him. Surprisingly, especially in Macnemara's case, for he was a black-hearted brawler who exemplified the dark side of Maryland, the side which felt comfortable with crime, instinctively approved of lynching, and made Baltimore "Mob Town." Cresap, violent but not vicious, proved to be the essential frontiersman for Maryland, fearing no authority and faring gladly to the western edge of civilization. A pair of Toms, both part of colonial Maryland.

A decade after he disembarked Dulany was on the way to eminence. One sign was that he had his portrait painted. In oils, no less, probably by the German immigrant artist Justus Kuhn, who before his death in 1717 painted Annapolis worthies almost by the dozen. Under his powdered peruke Dulany's face looks youthfully smooth though we note the forecast of a double chin. He surveys us indifferently, as if he were a born aristocrat. Yet Kuhn has caught in the cool brown eyes and the hint of a calculating smile something of the upstart vigor with which Dulany took on the world and made it—Chesapeake, forgive us—his oyster.

He rose to eminence by tying his own growth to the colony's. He came over as a redemptioner. That meant that he had to redeem the cost of his passage either by letting the ship's captain sell his services on arrival to some planter or by making the arrangements himself. Either way it was a hazard but so was the passage itself. It could easily take ten weeks to cross the Atlantic, and each week the dwindling food grew more maggoty and the filth below decks mounted. Though we can find few figures it's probable that in the early eighteenth century three out of every ten redemptioners and indentured servants died either during the passage or not long afterward. For awaiting them often were dawn-to-dusk drudgery in the fields and new American diseases like malaria. The planters politely called the process of survival "seasoning."

A small square-rigger carried Dulany in spring 1703 from England to the capes of the Chesapeake. Aubrey Land tells his story in an admirable book, *The Dulanys of Maryland*. Scarcely eighteen he came in the company of his two older brothers. What happened to them we don't know. If they survived their seasoning they merged into the growing mass of Marylanders: the field hands, the houseworkers, the artisans whose history is only beginning to be recovered. But we know about Daniel. After docking at Port Tobacco on the Potomac River, he promptly found his planter. Col. George Plater had doubtless ridden over—a Marylander never walked when he could ride—to purchase some help. The stocky Irish youth he took on for a four-year term was clearly a bargain. Unlike his brothers he had a bit of university education. For reasons that are cloudy to us, he'd left Dublin's Trinity College to strike out on his own. In exchange for the passage money which Plater paid the ship's captain he got a man who could be doubly useful. He could use

Dulany as a clerk in his law practice, for the colonel was a lawyer who had already been attorney general for the province; and he could use him as a bookkeeper for his plantation.

Beyond doubt the colonel benefited from the four years and Dulany benefited more. Plater probably kept his office, both for legal and plantation matters, in his house. If so Dulany received his training there in the two areas most important to an ambitious young Marylander, law and tobacco farming. For Dulany the first soon afforded a golden key to the second.

At the time he commenced clerking, Maryland justice was still rough and tumble. The colonial administrators of English laws and English procedures had faltered in the face of colonial conditions and then scrambled to adapt themselves. There was no code of laws, no body of precedents, no formal legal training. But there was abundant litigation in the overburdened courts, especially about land. Accordingly, many a planter, with a handbook like Michael Dalton's *Country Justice* open before him, made himself a lawyer. Or in his youth apprenticed himself briefly to a practicing attorney. A small group of such attorneys existed, who plodded over the court circuits and earned a living at the bar. They had more experience than their paralegal brothers but, aside from the handful who had studied law in London, no better training. Moreover, most of the judges were themselves laymen.

Though the colony officially boasted a quartet of superior courts—provincial, chancery, appeals, and vice-admiralty—the main action lay in the turbulent county courts. Their judges might have been amateurs but still they had manifold problems to cope with, and not only litigation about land. The county courthouses were small, jerry-built wooden structures; but they were often jammed with judges, lawyers, litigants, jurors, clerks, and interested observers.

Among other things the county courts appointed the overseers of the public roads. When the roads got so bad that wagons mired in them and horses foundered, the courts heard the inevitable complaints. The courts paid some attention to the welfare of orphans, although by the 1660s the orphans' courts, which survive even today, took over most of that responsibility. The courts paid out bounties for killing such pests to farming as squirrels and crows as well as for thinning Maryland's wolf packs. The courts directed the medical care, at least in rudimentary form, of the poor. They oversaw the keeping of county records: of births, deaths, and marriages; and of land contracts. They had the power to apportion local taxes and to spend part themselves; they did both. They set the rates charged by the little crossroads inns for housing guests and stabling horses; they even fixed the price of the food and drink served at the inns.

But these responsibilities, though wide, were only in addition to the principal business, which was to deal out civil and criminal justice. The civil statutes resembled those of today but the criminal ones look harsh to us. True, their rigors were relaxed for the rich but the poor got stern treatment, especially if they were indentured. And the women got worse treatment than the men, especially in sex cases. The Talbot County records for the final decade of the seventeenth century furnish a perfect example: "Jane Tomlinson, servant to Dr. James Benson, accused of having a bastard child and being thereof convict, it is therefore ordered by the court that the said Jane be carried to the public whipping post and there to have thirty lashes well laid upon her bare back by the sheriff." [1] Though typically the man involved wasn't whipped, the woman was not only whipped but sentenced to additional service to make up the time she'd lost by childbearing.

Dulany learned the law, and its rigors, with phenomenal speed and thoroughness. Because a register of legal precedents didn't exist, he dipped his quill and set down in his notebooks the decisions in court cases he had a chance to observe. He kept up this systematic recording for the rest of his professional life. By March 1707 he ended his indenture. By October Colonel Plater was dead and Dulany had lost his most influential friend. Probably the colonel gave him gifts like law books before he died.[2] At the least he must have given him the "freedom dues"

1. Quoted from Lois Green Carr's notes on these records, Hall of Records, Annapolis. Used with permission.

2. Letter, Aubrey Land to Bode, September 24, 1976.

he had coming, the bonus fixed by Maryland law. The dues at that time were a good suit of kersey or broadcloth, a shift of white linen, a new pair of stockings and shoes, and a new hat; also two hoes, one axe, and three barrels of corn.

By summer 1709 he was admitted to the bar of the county where he lived, Charles County. And he doubtless bought a wig, probably a brown bob one, the cheapest and most popular among the neophyte lawyers. There was much less legal ritual in Maryland than in England, but there was some and thereafter Dulany appeared in court bewigged.

Patently promising, he found several cases to handle during his very first term, the August term, and won them. His reputation grew with his practice and his next year, 1710, was studded with accomplishments. Of the five cases, for instance, that he handled during the August 1710 term, he won four. Then and in the following few years he took all kinds of cases but preferred civil to criminal because most of the civil cases dealt with land. In October he was admitted to practice before one of the superior courts in Annapolis, the provincial court. For cases in the county court the fixed fee he was allowed was 100 pounds of tobacco—the colony's common tender; but in the provincial court it was four times that. This same year he wangled his first government job, clerk to the house of delegates' committee on laws. For his labors, chiefly during the eleven-day official session, he earned 2,880 pounds of tobacco, or about £14 sterling.

During his brief stay in Annapolis he impressed the attorney general, William Bladen, who named him clerk of the indictments and prosecutor of Her Majesty's pleas for both Charles County and neighboring St. Marys. He set about his new duties with dispatch and during the time left over he pushed ahead with his private practice. No doubt he felt he had to. Serving the crown paid him more in prestige than money; and, though still a bachelor with slender responsibilities, he thirsted for money and what it could bring. He saw that the best opportunity to get it lay in land.

In Charles County, where he'd disembarked, and in St. Marys to the south of it, the best land was already owned by planters like Colonel Plater. So was the second best. However, in Prince Georges, to the west and north, only part of the best land had been taken though that was good indeed. An index to the resulting prosperity of Prince Georges planters was that in 1710 they owned more slaves per master than the planters of any other county. The fringes of the broad Potomac and narrower Patuxent had been unevenly settled, and wide stretches between hadn't been settled at all. These and more were there almost for the taking. Dulany's imagination was clearly kindled by a county so vast that its northern and western boundaries were only half defined, a vastness which touched Pennsylvania and Virginia, and which promised in valley after valley rich farms and lush meadows. Though nearly every planter could see only tobacco, Dulany had the wit to realize that other crops existed in the cosmos and that some of them might flourish in the far reaches of Prince Georges.

But that was for the future. Meanwhile Maryland had a single-crop economy and that crop was tobacco. Charles I was said to have remarked dryly that Virginia was "founded upon smoke"; so was Maryland. Over the decades tobacco yielded rich profits. But it devoured land. The use of fertilizers to replace the nitrogen and potash which tobacco drew from the red Maryland clay was unheard of. As a rule the earth was exhausted after four growing seasons and the planters moved cheerfully to other acres they owned. What they didn't own already they could often buy for a pittance.

Tobacco reigned with an absolute rule a Charles I could have envied. Smoking was widespread; any sketch of Maryland males was apt to show them puffing on "church-wardens," their long-stemmed clay pipes. It must have seemed almost disloyal not to smoke. And careless of one's health. John Josselyn, in *An Account of Two Voyages* (1674), observed helpfully that tobacco aided digestion, eased the pain of gout and toothache, cured coughing of the lungs, restored spent spirits, and killed nits and lice. He wasn't even a Marylander.

Tobacco continued to be the chief export to England. The plantations on the lowlands by Chesapeake Bay and the Potomac River were the best places to grow it. Most planters had their own docks, and the little ships of that era had no trouble in taking on the hogsheads of oronoco leaf or sweet-scented. The heavy labor needed to cultivate the crop came increasingly from black slaves. The white servants, even the convicts among them, were temporary help and exhaustible, and there was no such thing as white "hired hands" in the fields. The result was a slave economy, with no artisan or shopkeeping lower-middle class, with no towns of any size, but with plantations which were often rudimentary villages, self-contained and self-supporting. Whatever the planter, his family, and his plantation needed he could get more easily by ship from across the Atlantic than by land from fifty miles away.

Keenly aware that land meant profits and prestige, Dulany doubled his efforts to earn the money for it. He rode his horse, often no doubt with law books tucked in his saddlebags, tirelessly over the rough roads of the southern circuit, the one made up of Charles, St. Marys, Prince Georges, and Calvert counties. In a few busy years he became its leading attorney. Soon he was earning the equivalent of £100 sterling each year on the circuit and was practicing sporadically in each of the higher courts which lured him with their higher fees.

But it would be a caricature to picture him as obsessed with money. He relished life. His energy was so overflowing—he never fell ill—that he could spend his days on cases but his nights, or many of them at any rate, in the hearty, hard-drinking company of his fellow attorneys and the planters they counseled. An increasingly eligible bachelor, he probably had no trouble in finding a wife in the planters' families he got to know. He wooed and won a young woman named Charity Courts Smallwood, the daughter of one wealthy planter and the widow of another.

Along with a winsome wife Dulany gained his entrance into the planter class through Charity's family connections and ample dowry. He moved without effort into the landholding society of southern Maryland; doors opened smoothly. He now had still more in common with the planters because he managed Charity's two fertile plantations, Martin's Freehold on the Potomac and Hargage's Hope, a short distance inland.

Suddenly Charity was taken sick and died, at the end of

1711, after only a twelve-month marriage. By January Dulany was filing bond as executor of her estate. For a year he'd enjoyed a glimpse of the future, of wealth and power and of the meaning of marriage and married love. Now he was landless, since Charity's plantations had been entailed and so reverted to her family, and alone. In a symbolic gesture he moved from Port Tobacco to Nottingham Town, from Charles County to Prince Georges.

2. Plantations and Power

Though Nottingham Town was nothing but a hamlet, it had advantages for him, especially in location. It lay at the head of the Patuxent's estuary, halfway between Annapolis and Port Tobacco, within a day's horseback ride of either place. Charles Town, the county seat of Prince Georges, could be reached in little more than a couple of hours. More and more of his business was either in Annapolis or Charles Town; both places proved to be plums. By 1715 he handled as many as sixty or seventy cases during a single term of the provincial court in Annapolis. As early as 1712 he appeared as joint counsel in a case before the colony's highest court, the court of appeals; by 1714 he was beginning to appear as sole counsel. And the county court business in Prince Georges expanded so that it filled almost every remaining nook and cranny. But not quite all. For he also found time to buy his first plantation and to court the girl who became his second wife.

Brooke's Reserve near Nottingham was the plantation. In June 1715 he paid out £50 sterling and 2,000 pounds of tobacco for its 178 acres of tillable land, along with a house and farm buildings. In August he bought a second plantation, called Chance, along with 400 acres more from Charity's brother, John Courts. Now he ranked as a landowner and his little world acknowledged it. For one thing he officially joined the gentry. Before he was marked in the court records merely as Mr. Dulany; now he was Daniel Dulany of Prince Georges County, gentleman. Now he had his own servants to till his acres. By 1719 he had a total of nineteen blacks and indentured whites. Among those whose services he gained in one way or another, he couldn't find another Daniel Dulany. But he was able to hire an ideal overseer fairly soon for his expanding plantations, one Thomas Lawson, who went on to work for him for many years and eased his life immeasurably.

He put his increasing income into land. Bodkin's Quarter, 240 acres adjoining his residence in Nottingham. Stoke, 100 acres just off the Patuxent. Then he ventured farther away. Charles Bounty, 1,000 acres in Baltimore County. Remains of My Lord's Gracious Grant, 5,000 acres in Kent County. The roll lengthened each year in monotonous splendor. By the end of 1720 he estimated that he owned 27,200 acres. He was then, at the age of thirty-five, one of the largest landholders in the entire colony. Apparently his ambition was to be the largest.

Two years after Charity's death Dulany married again. Again he married a planter's daughter, Rebecca Smith, a good ten years younger than he, and a member of a large, well-connected, and well-off Prince Georges family. We know neither the details of the courtship nor the wedding day. About her dowry we know only that it included a plantation called Aldermason. Doubtless she had the unmarked vitality of youth when Dulany married her; doubtless she made a good wife and mother. On June 22, 1722 she performed what the era regarded as her most signal service: she bore a son, Daniel, Jr., destined to be as prominent as his father.

Though Dulany added readily to his acres, the role of plantation manager, as opposed to owner, made him yawn. He didn't care for its cycle of rural duties; he declined to be tied to the earth. So he depended more and more on Lawson, his gem of an overseer. That left him freer to do his legal work and to move around. As he rose in the Maryland bar, he had more cases in Annapolis. He relished going there. The little capital was expanding while he watched it. More of the colony's officials were either living in Annapolis or planning to. Affluent families were putting up red-brick houses, some of them quite handsome with their white trim and cool green or blue interiors. Social events were multiplying; there were balls, dinners, festivals, even wakes. There was much good eating, especially of Chesapeake seafood, and hard drinking, especially of rum.

Dulany began to feel that he was rusticating in Nottingham.

Why not live in Annapolis? It was easier because he already owned property there. With his usual foresight he'd bought a spacious, triangular plot of ground near the center of the town. Solomon Stoddert's plan of Annapolis, drawn in July 1718, shows it with his name attached. In late 1720 the Dulanys stepped onto Annapolis's grander stage. They probably built a house of the usual red brick, with a gambrel roof perhaps. They must have kept a coach to bump along the ruts in Annapolis and beyond. They certainly had a group of servants to run the house and ease the entertaining.

He found friends and patrons waiting for him. William Bladen, for instance, who owned a dozen lots, according to Stoddert's plan; and the leading Roman Catholic layman in the province, Charles Carroll, called "the Settler" to distinguish him from other later and eminent Marylanders of the same name. He was the wealthiest landowner in the province—characteristically he owned more of Annapolis than anybody else—and he employed Dulany to do a good deal of legal work for him. There was also one friend, far from a patron, who owned a pair of lots: Tom Macnemara.

In Annapolis Dulany's reputation continued its rise. He and Rebecca became almost at once leaders in the local society. In addition he was honored in spring 1721 by election to the vestry of Saint Annes. This was a solid stamp of approval. In a decade and a half Saint Annes had developed into the principal parish of the established Anglican church in Maryland. The single-storey building was a modest one, but the worshippers in it regularly included the governor and various other officials.

As his interest in planting waned, his interest in politics grew. He was, as the saying goes, a born politician. He evidently dealt well with men from the first time we hear of him. Moreover, as the years passed, he showed himself to be a thoughtful citizen who pondered political issues and reflected on the political process. His earliest office, clerk of the indictments, was that of a functionary rather than of a politician. But he gradually raised his sights.

Today we think of politics largely in terms of elections. Not in eighteenth-century Maryland; there the way to office lay more often through appointment than election, and appointment especially by the governor. From the start there had been an elected assembly—the charter had specified it, George Alsop had boasted of it—but its power swelled slowly. What Dulany hoped for at this time in his career was a sinecure of some importance. However, he was no trimmer and unfortunately he'd antagonized testy Gov. John Hart, who ruled from 1714 to 1720, by opposing some of his policies and working for Charles Carroll the Settler, one of Hart's main opponents in the colony. Dulany decided that he had better look elsewhere for help in his advancement, perhaps to London; what he couldn't get from Governor Hart he might get from Lord Baltimore.

He sailed in fall 1716 on a ship loaded with the usual hogsheads of tobacco. His stay in England had two practical results. One was that he was able to arrange for a sinecure, if only a minor one, the post of collector of customs for the North Potomac district, worth about £60 sterling a year. Whether that came through Lord Baltimore we don't know. The other was more satisfying. He secured admission to Gray's Inn, one of the four Inns of Court which provided the foundation for the British legal establishment. He signed its register on February 20, 1717, and then sailed back to Maryland a certified lawyer.

By January 1719 he lost the customs post but it didn't matter. He continued to dominate the southern circuit and he began to dominate the higher courts. Particularly the provincial court, where even before he became a Gray's Inn bencher he often had sixty or more cases on the docket during a single session. Between cases he purchased more plantations. He also purchased enough "warrants" from the colony's land office to give him an option on 14,500 acres more, anywhere in the colony.

His remarkable energy and acumen brought him a series of successes during the second decade of the century. He looks to us like a man of extraordinary shrewdness. Until we confront the fact of his devotion to Tom Macnemara, which was never anything but an embarrassment and a handicap.

We're not sure when they first became friends, but they both sailed here in the same convoy in 1703 although not aboard the same ship. Like Dulany, Macnemara found a Marylander to take over his services and pay for his passage. It was Charles Carroll the Settler. He introduced Macnemara into his household as a law clerk and Macnemara reciprocated by seducing Carroll's niece. Discovered, he married her. Marriage made no difference in his conduct. He showed himself to be a greedy, insolent bully but a bully with brains. He got himself admitted to the county bar even before Dulany and then got himself into one scrape after another. In 1706 he and another hotheaded attorney so bitterly abused each other in court that they were fined 100 pounds of tobacco. In 1707 he was kept out of the newly formed official bar of Maryland though he pushed his way in later. Even his occasional promises of repentance must have sounded insolent. Gov. John Seymour, Governor Hart's predecessor, once sentenced him to the stocks for an hour with his breeches off. If Seymour hoped that the humiliation would subdue Macnemara he couldn't have been more mistaken.

Instead Macnemara's conduct grew outrageous. He raped a woman in the Calvert County Courthouse. In another case he committed sodomy and plea-bargained his way to a charge of assault and a fine of 1,500 pounds of tobacco. In still another he and a companion were charged with beating a boatman so severely that he died. Macnemara threw himself on the mercy of the court and escaped with nothing but a branded *M*, for murderer, on his thumb.

This was Dulany's dearest friend. If we allow ourselves some psychologizing we can see Dulany responding unconsciously to the man's wicked and wanton proclivities. From the sexual assaults to homicide, his deeds were heinous. Yet Dulany readily shared cases with Macnemara even though his ill fame could prejudice the results. When Dulany sailed to London, Macnemara went along. When, after their return, he suffered one of his periodic disbarments Dulany took over all his cases—no light burden since Macnemara's practice was large. And when he died in 1720, Dulany accepted the responsibility for his son's education and guaranteed the administrator's bond of £3,000 for his widow.

Dulany was relieved of another burden besides Macnemara when Governor Hart left office. For a few months in 1720

Thomas Brooke, president of the governor's council, took over and then in late summer the new governor, Charles Calvert, arrived from England. He soon proved himself more of a diplomat than Hart. He needed to be, for he intended to restore the Calvert family's proprietorship to as much of its old power as possible. The crown had taken that power from the Catholic Calverts in 1689 after the Protestant couple, William and Mary, ascended to the English throne. The Calverts had made more than one effort to get it back; but it wasn't till 1715, after the current Lord Baltimore had renounced his Catholicism, that the new monarch, George I, restored to them most though not all of the power. Governor Hart, who'd arrived the year before as the crown's governor, tried to assert the proprietor's power as much as he had the crown's. He ran into stiff opposition, however. The colony had already enjoyed its taste of relative independence. Between the death of Governor Seymour in 1709 and the advent of Governor Hart in 1714, the crown had relaxed its supervision and allowed a Maryland magistrate, Col. Edward Lloyd, to preside over the colony. Even Brooke's brief tenure reminded Marylanders of the pleasures of self-government.

Though Governor Calvert took a benign tone toward the colonists, his basic position turned out to be much like his predecessor's. In his maiden speech to the assembly, he announced that the proprietor hoped to have with the good people of Maryland the relationship of a "bountiful, indulgent father towards a dutiful, deserving son." No doubt some of his hearers, in their seats at the state house, sat up at that; for they included a substantial party of independent-minded Marylanders.

The assembly had two bodies; the upper one was the council, appointed by the governor, and the lower one was the elected house of delegates. From early days their positions had been what we would expect. Most if not all council members, like the British Tories, upheld the principle of proprietory prerogative. They loved a lord. Most but certainly not all delegates, like the British Whigs, upheld the idea of a strong elected parliament. Beneath the politeness and eighteenth-century ceremony, the bobbing periwigs and the bows, the issue gradually hardened. Who would rule Maryland, the colonists or the proprietor? The colony was developing with a vigor which made authoritarian rule harder and harder to impose, especially from across the Atlantic. The movement which led, if half-consciously, to the American Revolution fifty years later was already getting under way along the Chesapeake.

In view of Dulany's achievements it was inevitable that he became involved in provincial politics. In the late summer of 1721 he ran for the Annapolis Common Council. The running meant more of a personal commitment than we might think, for the candidates had to stand near the polls while their neighbors, by voice vote, announced the man they preferred. Liquor flowed generously; the atmosphere was often raucous. Regardless, Dulany won. The office though modest had two advantages: its tenure was for life and it could be a step toward higher posts.

Though usually tactful, Calvert could also be touchy. Because of some quarrelsome misunderstandings with his attorney general, Thomas Bordley, he discharged him shortly after Dulany's election. Dulany was the only lawyer in the colony with a reputation as good as that of the widely respected Bordley, so Calvert offered the post to him. Dulany accepted, probably seeing to begin with no danger of a conflict of interest. He now became one of the senior officials of the colony, acting not only as the legal adviser of the proprietorship but as a policy maker. Like today's lawyers he was asked for advice on more than statutes; and he was more than a prosecuting attorney. In legal cases where politics was concerned, he may have found his role anomalous later on. But in prosecuting criminal cases, whether involving persons or property, he simply followed the stern pattern of his age. In April 1723, for example, he prosecuted an indentured servant named Mary Reed for stealing a small assortment of goods including a nightgown. This was grand larceny; she was sentenced to hang.

He was equally forthright when it came to more difficult criminal prosecutions. For instance, his prosecution of an Eastern Shore mob, one of many mobs during the next three centuries, for attacking a judge and the sheriff of Kent County when they went to the shore to enforce an unpopular order.

Dulany gathered enough evidence to convict the leader of the mob and a half-dozen of his gang. They were fined and two of the worst offenders whipped.

Two months after making him attorney general the governor made him one of the commissary generals and consequently a judge. The commissary general's court handled the probating of wills and the administration of estates, both subjects Dulany knew inside and out. It also handled land titles and his interest in those was profound. He had every reason to be gratified.

Vignette: Minority Report

To view Maryland through Dulany's bright eyes is to see a place of pulse-quickening promise, a colony which already rewards energy and foresight generously. To view Maryland through George Alsop's rose-tinted spectacles is to see Eden before the Fall. So, to widen our vision, we ought at least to take into account Ebenezer Cooke, the mock poet laureate and H. L. Mencken of our early eighteenth century. How does Maryland look to him?

We can find out most about him from Edward Cohen's *Ebenezer Cooke: The Sot-Weed Canon* though we shouldn't forget John Barth's big, mordantly comic novel *The Sot-Weed Factor,* whose title and topic he took from Cooke. We encounter Cooke in Maryland by 1694, at work for his father, a London merchant who dabbled in the tidewater tobacco trade and owned property in Dorchester County. He left the property on his death, probably in late 1711, to Ebenezer. In the early 1720s Ebenezer acted as a collection agent for the proprietor; in 1728 he was admitted to the bar of Prince Georges County. He probably died in 1733.

But he's not remembered for any of this. He's remembered for his rowdy verse-satires. The most notorious is *The Sot-Weed Factor,* which he published in London in 1708. The sot-weed of the title was the ubiquitous tobacco; the factor was a merchant. The poem covers more than twenty pages and is made up of clanging couplets with four beats to a line.

At the opening of the poem the factor has arrived in Piscataway from England with a stock of English goods to trade for

tobacco. At the close of the poem he heartily curses Maryland:
"May wrath divine then lay those regions waste/ Where no
man's faithful, nor a woman chaste." In between he's repeatedly overwhelmed by our boisterous colonials. His misadven-
tures are various. They include sleeping at a flea-infested inn
and finding the next day that his shoes, stockings, hat, and wig
have been thrown into the fire; suffering from chills and fever,
which he realizes is part of Maryland's noxious "seasoning";
and being gulled out of all his goods by a canting, thieving
Quaker.

Through the poem move half-dressed planters, sluttish
women, and drunken lawyers and judges. The planters wear
only shirts and drawers as they caper about. The women,
whether indentured servants or planters' wives, are fit for nothing but labor in the fields. As one angry female sneers at another:

> I knew you late a four-years slave;
> What if a planter's wife you go,
> Nature designed you for a hoe.

When our hero tries to sue his swindling Quaker he discovers
that the judges are bigoted sots, biased against outsiders. He
learns that, so far as justice is concerned, in the whole courthouse crowd "Not one amongst the numerous throng" ever
"has the heart/ To give his verdict on a stranger's part."

Nature itself stands against him in Maryland. Before leaving
for England he's menaced by rattlesnakes and periodically punc-
tured by mosquitoes. No wonder he embarks shaking a meta-
phorical fist at us.

3. Man of Maryland Affairs

Soon after Dulany settled into the job of attorney general he
ran again for elected office. The freeholders of Annapolis chose
him as one of their two delegates to the house. Although July
1722 was the time when the assembly was supposed to convene,
Gov. Charles Calvert wanted a postponement. Not sure that he
could get it legally, he called on his attorney general for an

opinion. He could, said Dulany, just as the kings of England could postpone the opening of Parliament. Dulany drew the parallel shrewdly, well aware that if a governor had the rights of a British king a colonist could maintain that he had the rights of a British subject.

Finally convened in October, the assembly got busy at once. The house made Dulany a member of its key committee on laws, the one he'd clerked for a dozen years earlier. The prime problem awaiting the committee at this session wasn't political but economic, the deregulation of tobacco. The highly controversial law then in force, dubbed the "trash act," banned the shipping of anything but clean tobacco to Britain. No frostbitten leaves, no suckers, no ground leaves. Though this pleased the big planters the small tobacco farmers unfortunately often had little but "trashy" tobacco to sell. The committee recommended repeal, to be followed by easier regulations. The house voted its agreement; the council refused to.

The house was wrathful at the rebuff. But it was also shrewd about it, or at least its leaders were; for they determined to use the tobacco issue as a step toward establishing their civil rights. It was something of a jump from tobacco to equal justice, but they managed it and embodied the result in what came to be called the "Resolutions of 1722." The main device the house proposed was both unexpected and ingenious. It was an addition to the oath the colony's judges took. It would make them swear to mete out justice to all, rich or poor, regardless of a governor's or king's displeasure. And it would make them try cases strictly according to English law and custom. Not surprisingly the council refused to endorse the resolutions; the proprietor rejected them. He wrote the assembly that though it could adopt specific English statutes it could never adopt English statute law in, as he put it, a lump.

The house then commissioned Dulany and two more members to search the records of the colony, even the dustiest, to show that English statute law had always been the basis of Maryland justice. Digging with zeal they unearthed ample evidence and in October 1724 Dulany, already known to be skilled with his pen, was invited to draft a new oath. He carefully kept the intention of the "Resolutions of 1722" but softened the language so artfully that the council hesitated to turn down this oath and the governor was undecided about it.

In his indecision he asked his attorney general for an opinion. Here Dulany clearly encountered a conflict of interest. He resolved it, with what satisfaction to himself we don't know, by deciding that the interests of the colonists and the proprietor agreed. He wrote to the governor that the oath wouldn't cut back the powers of the proprietor; indeed a good ruler would find his powers widened. The governor was reassured. The proprietor across the ocean, Lord Baltimore, was not. In fact, he was incensed. He considered that Dulany had turned into an enemy and set about to ruin him if he could. The proprietor's adherents helped to defeat Dulany when in the summer of 1725 he ran for re-election to the house. And the proprietors had the governor dismiss him from the post of attorney general.

For the next two years Dulany was fenced out of politics, whether elective or appointive. However, he had plenty to occupy him, including his law practice, his lands, and his emerging business ventures. He probably spent some time as well with his growing family. He certainly spent some time reading, particularly in the thorny field of political theory. He worked his way through the books, usually bound in the yellow calf which rubbed off on one's fingers, of such august thinkers as the Dutchman Hugo Grotius, who'd written *On the Law of Peace and War* a century earlier, and "the learned Mr. Locke" on civil government. Besides the theorists he read the English legal experts, Edward Coke and others.

This was reading with a purpose. The fruit of it and of much quill-scratching appeared in December 1728 as a thirty-one-page pamphlet, *The Right of the Inhabitants of Maryland to the Benefit of the English Laws.* His townsman William Parks printed it in his shop and sold it at two shillings a copy. The pamphlet turned out to be by far the most effective piece Dulany ever composed. It became the handbook of Maryland rights and even the revolutionists of fifty years later found it useful.

Its conversational tone and the range of its learning added to its effectiveness. In an era of heavy rhetoric Dulany had the sense to begin in an almost offhand way: "There has been a pretty warm contest concerning the right of the inhabitants of Maryland to the benefit of the English laws." He went on to develop a thesis with no surprises, that Marylanders were indeed Englishmen and so entitled to the protection of both English statute law and common law. But he supported it not only with Grotius, Locke, and Coke but with citations from Saint Paul, from Cato and Caesar, from the Magna Carta, and from parliamentary debates.

Though the success of his pamphlet gratified him, pamphleteering was a temporary occupation for him. Land development was not.

When he started buying land it was fundamentally for himself; those were his acres, his fields and farms. Now as the 1720s went along he moved smoothly into buying land to rent to others. Though the process was complex the rewards were rich. His first step was to buy warrants on vacant land from the proprietor. Then he had the choicest acres surveyed and, after paying an additional fee, had them "patented." Thereafter he searched for the most industrious tenants to till them.

Had he been shortsighted or greedy he would have charged them a high rent. However, he recognized that his land was useless without people to improve it. He made his leaseholds as alluring as he could, certain that even if he leased at a loss, he would gain later through the rise in value of the acreage he kept for himself. He cast a wide net for good tenants. He even advertised, on April 8, 1729, for example, in the *Maryland Gazette,* published in Annapolis by the same William Parks who had printed his pamphlet. He assured them that he would be as helpful as he could: "I will take the rent in tobacco, corn, wheat, or other produce of the land, which the tenants can best spare, at the price current, and give a reasonable time for making necessary improvements."

Prince Georges County continued to draw him into its vastness. Early in the decade he took a partner named John Bradford, who was both a planter in Prince Georges and a surveyor. They fixed on an area south and east of where the Monocacy River flows into the Potomac as their field of operations. Bradford laid out large tracts of fertile land along the Potomac, beyond the line of existing settlements. His reports were so glowing that Dulany determined to sell some of his property in the settled parts of Prince Georges so that he could invest in more lands along the upper Potomac.

Besides buying and leasing land Dulany went into other and diversified businesses. They reflected the growth of the whole colony. For one thing he became a money lender. The colony was always short of cash. The pound sterling rated as a treasured rarity; the pound of tobacco was far more common. In between lay paper money, a fluctuating currency viewed with suspicion by fiscal conservatives but kept in existence—indeed growing in use—because of the crying need for an easy medium of exchange. By law, sterling or its equivalent was required for remittances to the proprietor or to other colonies; and Dulany had a steady supply of sterling. It came partly from land transactions, partly from some London merchants he now did business with, and partly from some of his legal fees. He also had paper currency available and of course tobacco. He lent out all three, usually at 6 percent. He also joined in syndicates which bought and sold anything from ships to silver plate. One syndicate sold slaves. On May 20, 1729, the *Maryland Gazette* advertised that a ship had arrived in the South River with about 200 choice blacks, to be sold by Dulany and two other businessmen.

At the opposite extreme from the slave trade stood the most progressive and ultimately the most profitable of Dulany's business ventures, ironmaking. In it he proved as shrewd and enterprising as in land development.

The colonists craved iron, the most useful of metals. For its strength and hardness there was no substitute. They tried to improvise wooden tools, for example, but the results would have made an English artisan grin. For everything from axe heads to hinges they had to depend on English imports. And the more the colonists multiplied, the more iron they needed.

Maryland had the requisites: iron ore, often bog iron which lay on the surface of the earth and so didn't have to be mined; wood for the charcoal to burn in the smelting; and easy transportation by water. During the first quarter of the eighteenth century a few small ironworks which more or less satisfied these requirements went up in Pennsylvania, and in 1719 the Maryland Assembly passed an "Act for the Encouragement of an Iron Manufacture within this Province."

The idea fascinated Dulany. But what he heard about the problems of the Pennsylvania furnaces, as they called the smelters, made him cautious. No one in Maryland knew land and land values better than he, but about the production of iron he was as ignorant as any Prince Georges tobacco planter. So he proceeded to teach himself. Among the first things he learned was that to be successful the enterprise had to be extensive and consequently costly. Ironworking was no cottage industry. Reluctant to provide all the capital, he enlisted three of his wealthy Annapolis neighbors. They were the crusty physician Dr. Charles Carroll, the noted landowner and ex-mayor of Annapolis, Benjamin Tasker, and another Charles Carroll, son of the Settler. Later this Carroll was allowed to bring in his brother Daniel.

With Dulany they studied the problems and probable costs. They found a suitable site and in fall 1731 they formally organized as the Baltimore Company. Each of the five partners put in £700 sterling, making the company the most highly capitalized of any in Maryland. The site they bought was slightly above a point where Gwynn's Falls widened into the Middle Branch of the Patapsco River.

In the managing of the company the partners decided on collective control. From the outset it worked awkwardly but the chief reason it worked at all was Dulany's tact. He knew how to soothe irascible partners. In addition he took on the most troublesome responsibility while the ironworks was being erected, that of ensuring that the contractors did what they promised. Their workmen were often half-skilled and the contractors themselves often lazy or dishonest. We know that Dulany had to drag at least two of them to court for mounting the main wheelshaft in the forge so clumsily that it wouldn't turn. Nevertheless, construction was finally finished, and Dulany and his partners could look with pride on the pioneering plant.

The most striking building was the smelter, a tall cone of thick rock, with a bellows attached for the air blasts which the smelting needed. Nearby on the falls stood the forge, where the pig iron was pounded by water hammers into wrought iron. There was a coal house, to store the charcoal which the smelter consumed voraciously. There was a storage bin for the oyster shells which provided the limestone to carry off the impurities from the crude ore. And there were wooden barracks to house the indentured servants who supplied the main manpower.

A resident manager named Stephen Onion was hired. He turned out to be as efficient as Dulany's treasured overseer Tom Lawson, so the Gwynn's Falls works promptly showed a profit. Its operations were rarely trouble-free—the workmen got drunk and sometimes rioted—but within two years Onion could report that production was averaging fourteen tons of pig iron a week. Not only was there iron for the colonists but iron for export. In England the price of iron was rising, partly because the stores of charcoal there were being exhausted. With good contacts in London and Bristol, Dulany arranged for a full third of the English sales. Throughout the decades that followed, the works paid handsome dividends. For his initial £700 each partner received an average annual yield of £400. Thirty years after the works opened, each partner's share was valued at about £10,000. For them the ironworks was a gold mine. And the Maryland colonists got the iron for their hinges and hasps, their hoes and spiders, their nails and knockers.

More often perhaps than Americans imagine, the self-made man forgets his humble origins and identifies with the upper class he enters. Dulany certainly did, especially during the second half of his career. Once the opportunity arose, he went further and identified himself with the proprietor. However, the opportunity was tardy in coming. Governor Hart had viewed Dulany with resentment. Gov. Charles Calvert had become his friend but only after leaving office, though then the friendship grew close and Rebecca Dulany acted as godmother when Calvert's infant daughter Elizabeth was baptized at Saint Annes. Gov. Benedict Leonard Calvert, who succeeded him in autumn

1727, was an intelligent and educated young man, yet he never responded to Dulany's intelligence and acumen. That was the governor's loss; the colony had its problems and Dulany might have helped to assuage them. An important one was the tension in the assembly between the "country party," which represented the freeholders of the colony, and the "court party," which represented the interests of the proprietor. During Benedict Leonard's regime the tension grew. It grew so much that when he resigned because of ill health, the proprietor replaced him with a much different man.

He was the sharp-eyed, urbane Samuel Ogle. He soon saw at least one source of his predecessor's trouble. He wrote the proprietor to urge that an effort be made to soothe the feelings of such potent independents as Dulany and to win them for the court party. As it turned out, the proprietor himself had a chance to do it, for in the fall of 1732 the fifth Lord Baltimore made a state visit to Maryland. The visit proved to be the high point of the colony's history until then, with artillery banging away, bonfires at night, barrels of rum and gin, banquets with stupefying bills of fare, and candlelight balls where Maryland maids and matrons wore, over their stays, the richest brocade and finest lace.

But the proprietor hadn't crossed the Atlantic simply for sociability. He'd crossed because of a long drawn-out boundary dispute between Maryland and Pennsylvania. He'd let the heirs of William Penn cheat him out of mile after mile of Maryland territory by means of an altered map. Now he was trying to better a bad bargain by going to the scene. In addition he realized that some things had gone awry within his province as well as on its borders. Because he saw that even Ogle couldn't remedy conditions by himself, he made a point of exchanging views with various leaders among the colonists. He found Dulany especially impressive and soon gave him his confidence. In trusting Dulany he made no mistake; as it developed, Dulany spent the rest of his career gladly in the proprietor's service. Within eighteen months after Lord Baltimore sailed for home, Dulany was again attorney general and in addition judge of the court of the vice-admiralty and proprietary agent.

As attorney general he was the proprietor's lawyer; as proprietary agent, his tax collector. He embarked on his double duty with his customary vigor, with the sad but inevitable result that he lost friends in the country party. No doubt heads were shaken and eyebrows lifted, in Annapolis and elsewhere, at the sight of the author of the *Right* pamphlet putting all his talents to the proprietor's use. The colony's ambivalence about Dulany was nicely demonstrated in two things that happened in 1734. On the one hand the voters of Anne Arundel re-elected him to the house. On the other he became the victim of a whispering campaign accusing him of depreciating paper currency by giving less for it than for sterling. In summer he took to the *Gazette* to clear himself. There on July 19, 1734, he denied that he'd ever discounted paper money, saying, "I have always received, and always will readily receive it, equal to gold or silver."

He tried with his usual deftness to keep at least part of his effectiveness in the house. But the court party grew feebler while the country party grew more truculent. When Governor Ogle recommended to the house that it renew a tax for buying arms, it retorted by reprinting in its minutes the very "Resolutions of 1722" which Dulany had penned. When Dulany presented a claim for expenses incurred in the border dispute between Maryland and Pennsylvania, the house rebuffed him. It was hardly a surprise that before the decade ended he even lost his seat in the house, though there was irony in the fact that he lost it to one of his partners in the Baltimore Company, Dr. Charles Carroll.

In March 1737 Dulany suffered a harder blow than any which politics dealt him. Rebecca died, probably worn out as much by childbearing as by illness, as happened to many women. She'd had a baby on the average of every second or third year since the birth of Daniel, Jr., in 1722. Now with the birth of her last one, her health collapsed. Dulany and the children coped with the loss as best they could in their varied situations. Daniel, Jr., was being schooled at Eton in England; Walter, the middle son, was about to be apprenticed in Philadelphia; Dennis, the youngest son, was still a boy. Rebecca, named after her mother, and Rachel were old enough to assume some of the household responsibilities. Margaret was a ten-year-old while Mary, the youngest child, was an infant. How close the children were to their parents we can't be sure nor how close their parents were to each other. The family correspondence that has survived is dated too late for us to say. But it tells us that the older sons felt respect and affection for their father; their letters show it plainly. We can guess that there was a good deal of warmth in the Dulany household and that much of it radiated from Rebecca. We know that Dulany missed her and felt the need for a wife, for he remarried after a year; and that he had, at the least, no aversion to children, for his new wife was a young widow with six of her own.

She was Henrietta Lloyd Chew, the daughter of Philemon Lloyd, one-time secretary of the colony. The editor of the *Virginia Gazette* for September 29, 1738, characterized her with a bow as "an agreeable young gentlewoman with excellent qualities and a very plentiful fortune." His compliment wasn't empty. The marriage began well and continued well. For Dulany, now in his fifties, it may have lacked the ardor of the two previous ones; for it wasn't till four years after the wedding that Henrietta had her first child by him, a son they christened Lloyd. But the marriage obviously had abundant compensations.

4. The Maryland West

Ring-tailed roarers are rare in Maryland history. The colony's most splendid sample of the brawling, myth-making frontiersman was Tom Cresap, its own Daniel Boone, who pushed westward while Boone was still a baby. Cresap showed the same extravagant recklessness, though not the wickedness, which had drawn Dulany to Tom Macnemara. He came to Dulany's attention because of the proprietor's boundary dispute with Pennsylvania. By the time Dulany resumed office as attorney general, it had degenerated into a nasty little war, with skirmishes, bloodshed, and several deaths. In the mid-1730s he repeatedly rode the jolting coach to Philadelphia to defend Maryland's interest in general and certain Marylanders in particular. Chief among them, and most picturesque, was Cresap.

When Dulany saw him he sat defiantly in irons in a Philadelphia jail, a tough-fibered man. Then in his thirties, he lived to be ninety-six. He'd become involved in the dispute because the Maryland government had granted him 500 acres close to the broad Susquehanna River, about twenty-five miles into what is today Pennsylvania. The Pennsylvania authorities considered it to be in Pennsylvania then. Never inclined to yield to officials, especially if they were outsiders, Cresap got into a lively variety of clashes with them in the early 1730s. In his monograph on Cresap Kenneth Bailey describes many of these clashes. The one which sent him handcuffed to Philadelphia began in autumn 1736, when the Pennsylvania authorities issued a warrant for his arrest, charging him with nothing less than murder.

Following several abortive efforts to serve the warrant without bloodshed, the sheriff of Lancaster County collected two dozen armed Pennsylvanians and besieged Cresap's stoutly built log house. When the sheriff demanded his surrender—we still have the sheriff's report—"Cresap, with several horrid oaths and the most abusive language against the Proprietor and people of Pennsylvania, answered that they should never have him till he was a corpse." [1] They did have him, however, after setting fire to his log house. Shackled, he was marched through the streets of Philadelphia to jail. Along the way he gibed to one of the guards, "Damn it, Aston, this is one of the prettiest towns in Maryland." [2]

Dulany was unable to free Cresap though he got his irons taken off. During the next half-year Cresap remained so obnoxious that the Pennsylvania authorities entreated him to leave their jail and go home. He scornfully refused. It wasn't till a royal "cease-fire" proclamation arrived in August 1737 freeing the prisoners taken by both colonies—for Maryland had retaliated—that he let himself be released.

After his release he and Dulany became better acquainted. The Council of Pennsylvania had spoken indignantly in a letter to Dulany and a colleague about Cresap's "savageness of tem-

---

1. Kenneth Bailey, *Thomas Cresap: Maryland Frontiersman* (Boston: Christopher Publishing House, 1944), p. 49.
2. Bailey, *Cresap,* p. 52.

per'' and "daring resolution" but Dulany was probably attracted by both. Anyhow, Cresap was not nearly as savage as Macnemara, and daring resolution was exactly what Dulany was after. He still owned the warrants for hundreds of acres of land in western Prince Georges, still had his zest for speculation in those far reaches. But he needed help.

Once out of jail Cresap traveled purposefully westward, probably with Dulany's encouragement. There were two valleys he longed to explore in the Maryland West, one on either side of the Catoctin Mountains, the Monocacy Valley and the Antietam Valley. We don't know whether the Maryland government, mindful of his doughty services in the border war, gave him land outright or not. But in the late 1730s he patented a 550-acre tract on Antietam Creek, close to the Potomac. He christened it Long Meadow and built another of his stout log houses on it. That far west there were still many Indians and he tried his hand at fur trading with them. To finance it he mortgaged Long Meadow to Dulany for £500. However, he had bad luck with his fur trading. He had better luck with his land ventures.

In May 1740 he bought a tract about five miles from the junction of the north and south branches of the Potomac. Although less than fifty miles west of Long Meadow, it lay right on the Maryland frontier. Here Cresap settled in 1741 and made his permanent headquarters. He called the settlement Skipton after the Yorkshire town where he'd been born but others just called it Cresap's or, after a while, Old Town. It became the jumping-off place for voyagers into the wilderness. George Washington, who slept in a good many places, slept there more than once. He noted, for instance, in his diary for March 21, 1748, that he'd traveled all day "in a continued rain to Colonel Cresap's right against the mouth of the south branch." He added wryly that the road was the worst "that was ever trod by man or beast."

Throughout the early 1740s Cresap speculated in land on his own behalf and Dulany's. Dulany used him as he had John Bradford fifteen years before: as a scout for the best land, as a surveyor of it, and as an agent in selling much of it to others. Thanks to Cresap he now realized a profit on land warrants he'd taken up even in Bradford's time. And near the end of 1744 Dulany did something which deepened his personal involvement. He made an arduous journey into western Maryland to see it for himself. He came back enthralled. From then on he stood ready to buy land not only in acres but even in square miles. For example, in 1745 he acquired Tasker's Chance, which stretched for five miles along the Monocacy River on the east and extended westward to the foothills of the Catoctins.

Dulany was concentrating his speculations in a way that made most of his fellow speculators shake their heads. Because they were oriented toward tobacco growing, the lands they invested in had to be near water transportation. He was one of the few Marylanders to recognize how vital other crops, wheat in particular, were coming to be for a balanced economy; so he bought land which would be good for such crops, along with land which could be used for dairying.

Having gotten the land, first in the Monocacy Valley and then in the Antietam Valley, he looked around for settlers and found some practically waiting for him. They were Pennsylvania Dutch who were starting to move south because land cost less in that direction. Some traveled to the Shenandoah Valley in Virginia and beyond. Others proved to be ready to stop on the way, in Maryland. Many came originally from the Rhenish Palatinate in Germany. In the Monocacy Valley they saw lands which reminded them of those they'd left but whose cost was a pittance. By the time Dulany focused his interest on the area they were already to be seen here and there, farming, forming tiny communities, and founding their Lutheran and Reformed congregations. Though the loam of the Monocacy was rich enough, they discovered that the loam in the Antietam Valley was at times as thick as three feet. And in Dulany they met an owner ready to sell it to them at a loss.

He knew from experience with leasing that his losses at the outset would be more than made up by the added value of the land he retained. In the two years after buying Tasker's Chance he parceled out nearly 5,000 acres of it in farms of 100 to 300 acres and then sold them to the Pennsylvania Dutch for little more than a shilling an acre. The eyes of such men as Christian

Getzendanner and Joseph Brunner must have gleamed. So doubtless did Dulany's, for the Pennsylvania Dutch were demonstrably superior to most settlers. For instance, most when clearing land merely girdled the trees growing on it and then planted their crops around the dead trees. Not the Pennsylvania Dutch. They felled the trees, wrestled out the stumps, and then sowed, tilled, and reaped unimpeded.

A generation later, through the perspective of history, William Eddis neatly summed up the matter. An Englishman in the customs service at Annapolis, he mentioned Dulany and the settlements along the Monocacy in a letter of January 18, 1771. Dulany, he wrote, had been "much censured for having procured considerable tracts of lands in the vicinity of that river, which it was generally supposed could not even repay the trifling charge of the purchase for many succeeding generations. The richness of the soil and the salubrity of the air operated, however, very powerfully to promote population; but what chiefly tended to the advancement of settlements in this remote district was the arrival of many emigrants from the Palatinate and other Germanic states. These people who, from their earliest days, had been disciplined in habits of industry, sobriety, frugality, and patience were peculiarly fitted for the laborious occupations of felling timber, clearing land, and forming the first improvements; and the success which attended their efforts induced multitudes of their enterprising countrymen to abandon their native homes to enjoy the plenteous harvest which appeared to await their labors in the wild, uncultivated wastes of America." [3]

His lands were selling so well that Dulany foresaw the need for a town. He ordered it laid out on Carroll's Creek close to the Monocacy: 340 oblong lots, each 60 feet wide and between 350 and 400 feet deep, along with a small grid of streets. With a courtier's bow he called the new community Frederick Town after Lord Baltimore's son Frederick. Not that the compliment had any meaning to most of Dulany's customers, either in Fred-

---

3. William Eddis, *Letters from America,* ed. Aubrey Land (Cambridge: Harvard University Press, 1969), p. 51.

erick or in the surrounding area; for they bore names like Stumpf or Schultz and knew nothing about the Calvert family. Nor did the Scotch Irish or Welsh sprinkled among them.

In the spirit of toleration Dulany donated lots for the churches both of the Lutheran and the Reformed faiths. In May 1748 the Reformed minister Michael Schlatter could write: "On the 15th I preached in Fredericktown, in a new church, which is not yet finished. . . . After the sermon I administered the Holy Supper to ninety-seven members, baptized several aged persons and children, married three betrothed couples, and installed new elders and deacons." [4]

Always alert to new opportunities, Dulany got from Lord Baltimore a patent authorizing weekly markets in the town as well as yearly spring and fall fairs. He inaugurated them in 1747. They proved to be consistently if modestly profitable for him and a boon to the Monocacy area. Its farmers needed a place to sell their wheat and other crops and their well-fed cattle and sheep. Buyers and traders rode in promptly. Along with the fair came the usual cheerful relaxations, ranging from social gossip to horseracing.

The bustling farmers of the Monocacy soon demanded a government as close by as the market. Because they dealt most with the Prince Georges authorities, they had to travel the wearisome, meandering miles which led to the county seat at Charles Town. In 1745 and 1747 they tried to persuade the assembly to create a separate county for them but failed. However, in 1748, with Dulany captaining the campaign, Frederick County was voted into existence, with Frederick Town as the county seat. A shorn Prince Georges received boundaries much like those today but the boundaries of Frederick extended grandly to the western end of Maryland.

Busy though Dulany was with land, law, and politics, he couldn't forget that he had a family. As it grew older and larger it clamored for more of his attention. At times in the 1740s there were a dozen Dulanys and Chews, of assorted sizes, in his

4. Henry Harbaugh, *The Life of Rev. Michael Schlatter* (Philadelphia: Lindsay & Blakiston, 1857), p. 176.

Annapolis mansion. Although descriptions of the house itself are scant we can judge what it was like through the furnishings. The inventory when Dulany died testifies to the richness of the rooms. The dining room, for instance. It boasted of mahogany tables, of chairs with silken damask seats. Its sumptuous silver and glassware included eighty-nine syllabub glasses, for a favorite colonial drink of sweetened curdled milk, and sterling which weighed more than sixty pounds. Its cellar was stocked with everything from imported Madeira to Maryland-brewed Monocacy ale. And the household staff which Henrietta managed numbered no less than sixteen servants, black and white.

Though most of the family correspondence has vanished, here and there a late letter is preserved in the Dulany papers at the Maryland Historical Society; so here and there we can cast a bit of light on family matters.

On January 22, 1743, for instance, Daniel, Jr., sat down in his chambers at the Inns of Court in London and composed a long letter to his father. Underneath the eighteenth-century formality—it begins "Dear Sir" and ends, "That this may find you well is the sincere wish and hearty prayer of your ever dutiful son"—it looks familiar enough to us. For the dutiful son is explaining defensively that the rent for his chambers, £25 a year unfurnished, will seem high to his father but that it's really economical, it really is, to take them unfurnished and buy new furniture for them. But Daniel had little to worry about; his father was prepared to pay for the finest education for his talented son. He'd already sent him through Clare College in Cambridge, after Eton, and now was sending him through the Middle Temple at the Inns of Court for his legal training. And he was worth educating.

For his son Dennis, Dulany had hopes of a naval career. Young Daniel reports that he's learned the way to get Dennis started on it: he must be recommended by one of the lords of the Admiralty to the captain of a man-of-war. Luckily Lord Baltimore is one of those lords, so Daniel has waited on him and has politely asked for a letter on Dennis's behalf. Because Baltimore has agreed but hasn't sent it, Daniel writes that he plans to wait on him again.

Among Dulany's stepchildren was Sammy Chew, Henrietta's oldest boy. Daniel reports that he's in London, is well, and is getting ready to attend a school near London which Daniel has enrolled him in. Daniel assures his father that the headmaster is a sober, careful man and adds, with a modern concern for atmosphere, that the school "is situated in a very good air." Daniel also writes that he's done the business errands that his father wanted him to do. He drops in some London gossip to make the letter newsy, mentions a French defeat at Vienna, tells his father that he's sent him some magazines and newspapers, and gives him the compliments of ex-Governor and Mrs. Ogle, who had arrived in England on the same vessel he had.

Dulany's family was as expensive as his house. In clothing alone his wife, daughters, and stepdaughters cost him countless pounds for silks, satins, and brocades. His two oldest, Rebecca and Rachel, required before they married the elegant assortment of clothes which fitted their station; and eyebrows would have been raised in Annapolis if Henrietta hadn't dressed opulently. Even the boys cost money. We forget in our age of mass production that every piece of colonial clothing had to be made by hand. A tailor's bill among the Dulany letters evidences that. The Annapolis tailor John Campbell sent it to Dulany; it covers the two years between August 1747 and July 1749. In this period nearly all the charges are for clothing for his young stepsons.

We notice, for instance, that in August 1747 Campbell made two frocks for Master Sammy Chew; in September a coat, waistcoat, and breeches for Master Philemon Chew, his younger brother; and in November a jacket for Philemon and a vest for little Lloyd Dulany, then five years old. The rest of the bill is much the same, with pounds, shillings, and pence adding up steadily. Only the final charge, dated July 15, 1749, is for a coat Campbell made for Dulany himself.

Dulany wasn't stinting himself. He simply needed few new clothes by then. He traveled less and stayed home more, as he neared and then entered his sixties. Though he hadn't known a day of illness, as far as we can tell, he began to show his age in subtler ways. For example his handwriting became a bit crabbed in the reports he penned periodically to Lord Baltimore. On his death in December 1753 his wardrobe was divided among his widow and his two eldest sons. The list is preserved in the Dulany papers. The wardrobe is far away from the single suit of kersey or broadcloth due him from Colonel Plater on finishing his service.

Among the many items, to Henrietta went mostly the lighter ones such as shirts, nightcaps, stockings, and handkerchiefs as well as, perhaps for sentiment's sake, his brown bob wig. To Daniel, Jr., went the finest clothes, including a black velvet waistcoat and black velvet breeches, ruffled shirts, and black silk stockings. Dulany may have worn his black velvet on both official and social occasions, for it was standard dress when lawyers appeared before the colony's high courts. To Walter went what was left including an old bearskin coat, plenty of everyday linens, a gray bob wig, and a pair of spatterdashes—cloth gaiters Dulany had worn to shield his stockings from the Maryland mud.

By the time he died Dulany had spent half a century in Maryland and had helped the colony come of age—as a colony. Throughout the decades he'd been attuned to the colony and to the era. His gifted son Daniel would help the colony during some of the turbulent years before it became a state; but midway the currents of rebellion would sweep past him and after that, when it came to the shaping of the state and nation, he would be ignored. No one would ever be an emblem for the emerging state as Daniel Dulany the Elder was for the developing colony.

2

Tumult and Hoarse Shouting

5. Outdoor Politics

*T*HERE'S much to be said for the austere effort to write objective history, history from without. But there's at least a little to be said for writing history from within, especially where conflicts—above all, wars—are concerned. So for the next hundred years of Maryland history we'll turn at times to the state's two most noted nonobjective historians. The first is J. Thomas Scharf, a mustachioed veteran of the Confederate forces, who after the Civil War manufactured reams of Maryland history. He favored the South—naturally; the Democratic party—despite its blemishes; and the well-to-do—a Maryland capitalist made him beam. His chief works were the *Chronicles of Baltimore* (1874), *History of Maryland* (1879), *History of Baltimore City and County* (1881), and *History of Western Maryland* (1882). The second is Matthew Page Andrews. Born in West Virginia but a resident of Maryland all his adult life, he wrote his *History of Maryland* (1929) with the enthusiasm of a convert. To him, even in the twentieth century, Maryland was the best of all possible states and Marylanders the best of all possible persons. He wrote about the Revolutionary War as a patriot who couldn't quite smother the instincts of a loyalist and about the Civil War as if he'd quietly voted for Jeff Davis.

But it can be argued that their biases are useful because they

40

help to offset our own; and by their very difference from ours they can remind us that Maryland has long been a divided state. Consequently, they'll be quoted from time to time, though usually with a touch of caution.

Nobody knows exactly when a revolution starts but we might date the American one from the Stamp Act, which Parliament passed in London with a yawn in March 1765, to take effect half a year later. The yawn could be forgiven for it looked reasonable, even routine, to tax the colonists in order to pay for protecting their frontiers. Moreover, as Andrews murmured in a footnote, "The British people were paying a stamp tax, and the fact that the colonial tax was modeled after [it] made it seem just to the British proponents." [1] The colonists, though, were far from yawning; they were incensed at taxation without representation. Not only were their legal and official documents to be taxed but also their newspapers and even their playing cards. The stamp itself was embossed on blank sheets, on which the documents were to be prepared. Soon bales of sheets were being shipped to each colony and stamp distributors named to sell them.

Along with the other colonies Maryland simmered throughout the spring and summer months. In late August the colony found a scapegoat in the form of an Annapolis merchant named Zachariah Hood. While on business in London the luckless Hood had been appointed stamp distributor for Maryland by the crown. On August 22 the *Maryland Gazette,* which the printer Jonas Green had revived after William Parks let it lapse, printed a letter from London with the inflammatory news. A few days later a mob gathered in Annapolis, led by a hungry young politician named Samuel Chase. The mob concocted an effigy of Hood, carted it through the streets to the executioner's lot just outside of town, and there hanged and burned it. According to Andrews, Hood was also burned in effigy in Baltimore and Elk Ridge Landing. About this time his ship reached Annapolis but a mob prevented him from docking. As Andrews put it, vio-

1. Matthew Page Andrews, *History of Maryland: Province and State* (New York: Doubleday, Doran & Co., 1929), p. 277.

lence led to violence and at least one person was badly hurt. When Hood managed to disembark and return to Annapolis— he'd been looking for another place to dock—he found many hands raised against him, literally. He was roundly insulted and when he rented a small warehouse to store the stamps a mob pulled it apart. All this was part of what came to be called "outdoor politics."

The *Gazette*, moved by profit as well as principle, fed the fire. Among other things it published pointed warnings to "sycophants" and "cringing court politicians." Searching desperately for succor Hood fled to New York and relative safety. The episode won wide attention, one loyalist writing ruefully that he didn't want to be "Zak-Hooded." But after tempers cooled Hood was allowed to come back, partly because the emerging "Sons of Liberty" in New York had made him surrender his stamp commission. And the Maryland Assembly, with what some patriots regarded as excessive fairness, voted to reimburse Hood for the demolished warehouse and even to reimburse a carpenter who'd lost a chest of tools in the building.

The atmosphere was electric by late September 1765 when the assembly opened. Waiting for it was a fervent communication from the Massachusetts House urging it to make common cause with the other colonies by joining in a Stamp Act congress. The assembly quickly named three antitax activists and sent them north to oppose all taxation without representation. The delegates were Edward Tilghman of Queen Annes County, William Murdock of Prince Georges, and Thomas Ringgold of Kent. The congress met in New York City with delegates from seven other colonies besides Massachusetts and adopted a broad declaration of rights and grievances.

Back in Annapolis the foremost lawyer in the colony was preparing what proved to be a classic pamphlet on the act. It was Daniel Dulany the Younger, following in his father's footsteps. *The Considerations on the Propriety of Imposing Taxes in the British Colonies for the Purpose of Raising a Revenue by Act of Parliament* was printed in October at the office of the *Gazette*. Simplified and stripped of its quotations from Cato and the rest, Dulany's argument was that British subjects shouldn't be taxed without their consent and that the subjects in the colonies couldn't give consent since they weren't represented in Parliament. His pamphlet, like his father's *Right of the Inhabitants of Maryland to the Benefit of the English Laws,* was promptly and widely acclaimed. Though issued anonymously its author was soon recognized. The pamphlet circulated into New England and across the Atlantic, where the renowned William Pitt praised it in Parliament.

In the same month that Jonas Green printed *Considerations* he announced that he would suspend his journal rather than pay stamp duty. Actually, the paper went underground. On November 1, while church bells tolled and demonstrations occurred, the act took effect. On December 10 the *Gazette* surfaced to report that Frederick County, thanks to its liberty-loving magistrates, would go on with business as usual, ignoring the stamp tax on legal and commercial documents. The *Gazette* noted that the citizens had used what we now call street theater to display their defiance. It also qualified as "outdoor politics." They'd organized an elaborate procession. It had been headed by some citizens carrying flags and drums, followed by others waving banners with such inscriptions as "Magna Carta," "Oppression Removed," and "Liberty and Loyalty." A coffin had brought up the rear with the inscription on it: "The Stamp Act, expired on a mortal stab received from the genius of liberty in Frederick County Court, 23d November 1765." Zachariah Hood was represented in effigy, as the sole mourner.

The newly formed Sons of Liberty in Frederick County, under tough old Tom Cresap, were the most stalwart resisters of the act and provided a stimulating example to similar groups forming in Baltimore and in Anne Arundel County. In February 1766 the Baltimore group took it on itself to send Dulany a threatening letter because, as current secretary of the colony, he hadn't followed the example of Frederick County. To the demand that he reopen the courts throughout Maryland, he said no. Other officials didn't stand fast, however, and in the face of increasingly effective demonstrations the courts went back to work. The Sons of Liberty represented the forces of guerrilla warfare in these disputes just as Dulany represented the protests through the process of law. Doubtless both had some effect on Parliament; at any rate on March 18 it repealed the obnoxious act.

The ten years between 1766 and 1776 were ones of unevenly accelerating struggle. When Parliament repealed the Stamp Act it also noted frigidly that it reserved the right to legislate about the colonies "in all cases whatsoever." In 1767 it passed the Townshend Revenue Acts, named after the Chancellor of the Exchequer Charles Townshend, which taxed the tea, glass, paints, and paper imported throughout the colonies. In 1768 in response the colonists, led by the Sons of Liberty, decided to cut off trade with Britain. They revived associations of merchants who'd helped in the obstruction of the Stamp Act and urged them to boycott British goods. They also put pressure on unco-operative merchants or, as they called them, nonassociators or, as they also called them, "enemies of the liberty of the American people." The combined protests worked. In April 1770 the Townshend Acts were repealed by Parliament except for the tax on tea. The merchant associators in New York, Boston, and Philadelphia then softened their stand through a natural yearning to do business again. The Baltimore merchants felt that they could do the same. But when they tried they encountered opposition throughout the colony. A special convention in Annapolis in October denounced the action of the Baltimore merchants as inconsistent and even indecent.

Nevertheless, tensions relaxed between Maryland and the mother country. The Boston Massacre, so called, happened in March 1770 but the *Maryland Gazette* gave it small space. While Boston's Sam Adams made the most of its martyrs Marylanders turned back to their own affairs. For three years the *Gazette* carried little but provincial news. The assembly became preoccupied with a trio of vexing domestic issues. They were the amount of inspection tobacco should have before being exported, still a sore point; the source of fees for the colony's officials; and the reduction in the income of the often lazy or profligate Anglican ministers.

For three years the tensions relaxed but after that they in-

creased ominously. We can see both the initial calm and the en-
suing storm as they affected William Eddis, the Englishman
who'd praised the elder Dulany's foresight in investing in western lands. An impecunious Londoner with tastes beyond his
flattened purse—for instance, he loved theater-going—he managed to migrate to Maryland. In Gov. Robert Eden he acquired
a generous patron who had him appointed surveyor of customs
for the port of Annapolis. Eddis arrived in fall 1769 and was
soon introduced to the joys of colonial upper-class life under the
auspices of the governor. A perceptive correspondent, Eddis
wrote a series of letters home from then till fall 1777. Years afterward he polished and, to our advantage, published them. *Letters from America,* issued in London in 1792, offers us not only
an account of Eddis's career but the best picture we have of life
in and around Annapolis.

What does he tell us during the three-year lull, Londoner that
he is? Among other things, that the noble Chesapeake makes the
Thames look small . . . that Annapolis boasts more pretty
women than any comparable town in England . . . that the theater here is much more professional than he thought it would be
. . . that the deer, once said to be numerous, are being slaugh-
tered for their hides so wantonly that they're in danger of extinction . . . that little Baltimore has grown into "the grand empo-
rium of Maryland commerce" . . . that Frederick Town is
likewise flourishing; now larger than Annapolis, it has mostly
wooden buildings instead of brick, however . . . that the pursuit of pleasure is constant among the well-to-do; there are
horseraces, theater parties, dances, card games, dinners, sup-
pers, and a host of other occasions for a "cheerful glass". . . .

That land is easy to get through warrants; a hundred acres can
be secured for only a few pounds plus an annual quitrent of two
shillings . . . that Marylanders are busybodies, inquisitive
beyond the limits of English propriety: "there are few who do
not seem perfectly conversant with the general and particular interests of the community" . . . that Marylanders are democratic:
"the inferior order of people pay but little external respect to
those who occupy superior stations" . . . that in Frederick

County the farmers' life is rough by Annapolis standards: the houses are two-room log cabins; the main meal is hominy, with beef, pork, or bacon added from time to time; but fruit is plentiful, for most farms have apple and peach orchards. . . .

Eddis was in his unobtrusive way a diplomat. He managed to avoid damage by any of the three provincial controversies, even the one about fees for officials, and he carried out his appointed duties as surveyor of customs without any visits by wrathful Sons of Liberty. He continued to be welcomed in the houses of the gentry as he traveled around Maryland. "I am content and grateful," he declared in his letter of October 3, 1772.

A little more than a year later, through no fault of his, the Boston Tea party altered all that. The Bostonians dumped the tea in the harbor on the night of December 16, 1773, and the news stirred colonists everywhere. The event aroused Marylanders as the Boston Massacre never could. Eddis saw what was coming: "I view the impending storm with inexpressible inquietude," he wrote on January 3, 1774. And by the time he wrote his letter to Britain of May 28 he could cry, "All America is in a flame!"

The tumultuous events of the next three years have a local focus for us in his correspondence. He went on in the letter of May 28 to copy down the resolutions passed by a citizens' meeting a few days earlier. They stated that Boston was "now suffering in the common cause of America" because of the British order blockading its harbor, and that the people of Annapolis would join the effort to stop all trade with Britain, both import and export.

During the next months the position of the colony's activists stiffened. On October 26 Eddis described the *Peggy Stewart* affair, still commemorated today, which marked the revival of the violence and threats of violence of the Zachariah Hood episode.

The brig *Peggy Stewart*, owned by Anthony Stewart of Annapolis and named after his daughter, arrived from London on the 15th with 2,000 pounds of tea consigned to the Annapolis merchants Joseph and James Williams. An angry mob condemned the men harshly, the Williams brothers for ordering what the *Gazette* on the 20th termed "that detestable weed" and

Stewart for paying duty on it. Resentment swelled both in the town and in Anne Arundel County. A shaking Anthony Stewart made his way through successive stages of humiliation. He sought a meeting with the irate citizens; he was refused. He published a handbill with an elaborate explanation of his conduct; it was ignored. Then he and the Williamses were presented with a paper to sign. In it they confessed that they'd "committed a most daring insult" to the liberties of America; that they would never do it again; and that they would readily burn the detestable tea. They signed the paper. For the most militant of the citizenry this was still not enough. Finally Stewart, by no means sure that his life was safe, offered to board his brig and set fire to it, with all its cargo. In a few hours it burned to the waterline and the crowd was appeased. The threat of violence had been completely effective; outdoor politics had worked again.

On April 26, 1775, Eddis reports the news of the battles of Concord and Lexington, adding that he awaits further information with "the most dreadful anxiety." On July 25 he writes about the Battle of Bunker Hill and observes that Maryland is preparing for war. "In almost every district of this province the majority of the people are actually under arms; almost every hat is decorated with a cockade; and the churlish drum and fife are the only music of the times." On August 24 he announces the dismal discovery by neutrals in any revolution: "to be neuter is to be adverse." On September 26 he writes that he has given up his house and is staying at the governor's. On March 29, 1776, he reports a key event, the exit from Boston of the British forces and the entrance of Washington and his Continental troops.

By now "Committees of Observation" have been formed throughout Maryland under the authority of the Continental Congress. They're the actual government, even fixing the price of salt. Eddis writes in agitation on June 4 that the local committee has summoned him before it. No good course of conduct offers itself to him; the least bad is to return to Britain. A week later he has met with the committee and has been expelled from Maryland. On July 8 he writes, "The colonies, by their delegates in Congress, are declared free and independent states.

. . . I cannot but contemplate with horror the complicated miseries which appear ready to overwhelm this devoted country." A year later, after many delays and tedious preparations, he embarks for England. The first night on shipboard he stays up looking sadly at the receding Maryland shore till he can't see it any longer.

6. War Next Door

How dare we offer a history of Maryland which doesn't pay ample attention to the military campaigns of the Revolution? The answer is, it's easy. Not one battle was fought on Maryland soil. There were only a few small naval raids. The only time that British troops stirred up Maryland dust was when they marched from the head of the Elk River, having sailed up the Chesapeake in the summer of 1777, to the Delaware border on their way to besiege Philadelphia. Twelve miles.

It's true that inside the state many hours were spent in drilling, as Eddis says, and some in recruiting. And that outside the state our soldiers fought well and were rarely repulsed. "The achievements," Andrews noted, "of the distinctive and distinguished body of continental troops which came to be known as the Maryland Line began in the summer and fall of 1776." And those achievements continued till Cornwallis was cornered at Yorktown in the fall of 1781.

What we might do is take one man from the seven regiments which constituted the renowned Line and look at his career in the war. Perhaps William Beatty, Jr., who left us a brief, spotty, but useful journal.[1]

Scarcely eighteen when he left home in Frederick County to become an ensign in the army, he kept a record of his activities from June 25, 1776, to January 25, 1781. In early July 1776 he raised his quota of troops, probably sixteen men, and marched them to Philadelphia, where they were outfitted. He proved to be a young Stoic who never complained about the poor equipment he and his men received, but we know from other sources

1. "Journal of Capt. William Beatty. 1776–1781," *Maryland Historical Magazine* 3 (1908): 104–119.

that it was scant and shoddy indeed. For uniforms they probably had to make do with the clothes they had on. For weapons single-shot, smooth-bore muskets about five feet long. For cartridges twisted papers of black powder, which had to be bitten open, and leather cartridge boxes to contain them and the little lead balls the muskets fired. Their knapsacks were probably canvas, their blankets anything to keep out the cold. Their tents were A-shaped, ordinarily six and a half feet square, five feet high, and designed to huddle together five soldiers each. As the war went along, the issuing of equipment became more systematic but there was always a grim truth to the cliché about "the ragged Continentals."

Beatty next marched his men, stage by stage, to New York where they joined the Continental army gathering on Long Island. Luckily he arrived too late to share in the thumping defeat the British administered to General Washington's men. In mid-October he did something typical of the ill-supplied and ill-attended American troops: he got sick, probably from malaria. Being an officer he was able to leave his company for two weeks to recuperate near Hackensack. Returning he took part in the retreat through New Jersey. During it he equably recorded in his journal experiences pleasant and unpleasant. One night, for instance, he quartered at the home of a gentleman who treated him "with a great deal of politeness and hospitality." Another night he had to march his men over brutally rough roads—very hard duty, he noted. When the brigade he was in reached New Brunswick, it left the army to return to Maryland since its enlistment was over, the kind of thing which was happening in the Continental army all the time. He helped pay off the soldiers in Philadelphia and by mid-December was snugly home in Frederick County.

The result was that he missed the brilliantly managed battles which Washington won at Trenton and Princeton. But Beatty was no sunshine soldier; he soon re-entered the war by taking a commission as first lieutenant in the Continentals. Again he had to recruit his own troops. In June 1777 he led his company north into New Jersey to join the forces of, as he phrased it, "Our Hero." He reported in his journal of August 25 on the

British threat to his home state: "The army and fleet of the enemy being now in the Chesapeake Bay, the whole of our troops began to move that way." On September 11 he took part in the Battle of Brandywine, reporting dryly that "the enemy appeared and made a very brisk attack which put the whole of our right wing to flight."

Germantown was a bit better: "About sunrise [our] attack was made with such briskness that we had the pleasure to pursue the enemy entirely through Germantown." But then Lord Cornwallis marched up with reinforcements, "and some bad management on our side obliged us to retreat." When Washington took his army to winter quarters at Valley Forge but sent the Maryland division to Wilmington, Beatty admitted that the housing there was good. But he added that the Maryland troops were very bare of clothes. On June 8, 1778, he and his command rejoined Washington and the decimated Continentals at Valley Forge. On June 28 and 29 he saw action in the Battle of Monmouth, which ended when the British took "advantage of the moonshine about one o'clock the morning of the 29th and retreated to avoid the attack."

On July 4 in this half-organized war Beatty gained permission to travel to Cecil County, where he'd left some baggage. Having gotten it he hitchhiked a good part of his way back. "I left . . . on foot but after going about ten miles a gentleman overtook me who gave me a seat in a chaise to Bristol." Even after returning to his troops he went off every now and then. On July 30, for instance, he rode to some saw pits and dined on oysters; afterward he rode into Connecticut and sipped some good wine. On December 1 he and other officers who were lodging at a Mr. Jackson's in Chester "collected the girls in the neighborhood and had a kick-up in the evening."

Most of the winter of 1778–1779 he spent away from his company, where he'd been promoted to captain, and back in Maryland. During the summer of 1779 he and his men took part in the American victories at Stony Point and Paulus Hook. Then he was detailed to do recruiting again, so he passed the months between January and October 1780 first in Frederick County and then in Annapolis. In November he joined the massive movement of the American forces to the South. He returned to the Maryland Line on December 7 in Charlotte, North Carolina, having received command of a new company. The Americans advanced by slow stages through the interior of North Carolina into South Carolina. His company encamped near the Peedee River and on the night of January 12, 1781, he went hunting there. In his final journal entry, of January 25, he remarked once again that some of the militia had left, their enlistment being over.

Three months later came the Battle of Hobkirk's Hill. When leading a charge by a battalion of the Maryland Line, Beatty was killed by a musket ball in the forehead. His own company fell back; a retreat started; and the battle was lost. The battle was lost; but the war was won, only six months later, when Cornwallis surrendered at Yorktown.

Vignette: Transit

Between two wars the colony finished becoming a state. By 1782 peace was being negotiated. Maryland was already functioning under its first constitution, shrewdly framed in Annapolis by the wealthy for the wealthy and approved in 1776. Under it you had to own property to vote or hold office—as much as £5,000 if you yearned to be governor. Not that the governor wielded much power; the framers, fearful of a strong executive, hedged him in with a newly devised senate as well as a house of delegates and council. On the other hand the framers weren't merely jealous oligarchs. For all white-skinned Marylanders they provided a bill of rights with more than forty clauses. When the War of 1812 opened, the bill of rights remained but the property qualifications had been gradually erased.

On the national level Maryland functioned almost independently before 1782. It didn't sign the Articles of Confederation, adopted by Congress in 1777, till 1781. However, by 1812 it was getting used to being governed by the durable Constitution of the United States, which had been ratified in 1788. What constantly concerned Maryland and the other states was the proper extent of the governing. The Federalists argued for more government; the Anti-Federalists, later named the Republicans, insisted on less. The Federalists termed the Republicans congenital rebels; the Republicans stigmatized the Federalists as closet monarchists. Nationwide the Federalists lost out early. By 1812 they hadn't elected a president since John Adams, while the Republicans had elected Thomas Jefferson for two terms and James Madison for one—and were in the process of electing him for another. In Maryland, though, the battle between the parties seesawed because of the state's political complexity. The feuding came to a climax in the election of 1812 shortly after the war was declared. Republican mobs in Baltimore attacked Federalists so ferociously that they killed at least one and drew blood from many more.

Maryland's economy seesawed like its politics but that was chiefly because of world conditions, not local ones. Everything considered, the state did well between the wars. Especially in exports. A recession in 1786 interrupted their rise but otherwise it was impressive for a decade. For example, in 1794 exports amounted to more than $5,680,000; in 1799 they peaked at $16,300,000. President Jefferson dealt Maryland's economy a thudding blow in December 1807, when he put an embargo on exports to avoid having American shipping caught between an embattled Britain and France. The state's exports plummeted from $14,300,000 in 1807 to $2,700,000 in 1808. But the next year the embargo was lifted and from then till 1812 they averaged a good $6,000,000 annually.

The state's population rose more evenly than its exports. The fledgling federal census for 1790 counted 209,000 whites, 103,000 slaves, and 8,000 free blacks; and the one for 1810 counted 235,000 whites, 111,500 slaves, and 34,000 free blacks. As its port expanded, Baltimore outstripped the rest of the state. In 1790 it had only about 12,000 whites, 1,250 slaves, and 320 free blacks, but in 1810 it had 27,900 whites, 3,700 slaves, and 3,970 free blacks.

All this growth and change was momentous but life in Maryland contained more than momentousness. It contained, for instance, a considerable shift in fashions. If in 1782 you were a Maryland male you clung to the clothes of your fathers, including a three-cornered hat, a long open coat, a fancy waistcoat, knee breeches, and stockings. However, by 1812 you'd traded your tricorn for a tall hat with curved brim and your knee breeches for tight trousers. If you were female you wore, in 1782, a low-necked, narrow-waisted dress over a corset, with a full skirt over a hooped petticoat. But by 1812 you were making men's eyes glint. You'd shed corset and hoops, and over flimsy underclothes you now wore the high-waisted, flowing, and revealing "Empire" dress popularized by Napoleon's court. Though you sometimes shivered, you were in style.

7. War Aplenty

Though the Revolutionary War bypassed Maryland, the War of 1812 more than made up for that oversight. For two crowded years Maryland felt the pangs of plundering and conquest, heard the yells of victory, gave the groans of defeat. But it also felt the relief of survival, so we still celebrate Defenders' Day each September 12 to mark the Battle of Baltimore. And we still sing the anthem, though without remembering all the words, born from the same relief.

As the war with Britain neared, the state split about joining it. The majority sentiment was probably voiced by a committee with members from all over Baltimore which met on May 21, 1812, at the city's Fountain Inn, where in the past General Washington had been welcomed, and resolved that since the United States had the choice only "between war and degradation," it had to be war. A month later the war came, although for a time it spared Maryland. At the start the British were grappling with Napoleon and, moreover, concentrating in the Great Lakes region such North American forces as they had. But Maryland's turn arrived early in 1813.

Feisty George Cockburn's fleet of a dozen British fighting ships entered Chesapeake Bay in the first week of February and made itself at home. On admiralty orders, it set up a blockade of the Chesapeake in general and Baltimore in particular, a blockade which was to continue for a year and a half and prove so successful that the city's shipping trade would never fully recover. In April the fleet sailed slowly up the bay, menacing Annapolis and Baltimore as it went. It anchored at Elk River, at the head of the bay, and unleashed its marines to do as much damage as possible. At Havre de Grace early on the morning of May 3 they attacked not only with weapons which the ill-equipped Maryland militia had seen before but also with newly devised rockets, made and fired much like the mortars of today. The historian Jared Sparks, then an absentee sophomore from Harvard, contributed an eye-witness account, "Conflagration of Havre de Grace," to the *North American Review* of July 1817. He wrote that the rockets produced a great agitation and that when one of the militia was killed by a rocket the rest fled to the nearest woods. The British set fire to about forty of the town's sixty houses after ransacking these and more. They smashed mirrors and ripped open feather beds. The officers picked out tables and bureaus they liked, wrote their names on them, and had them put aboard the British barges. Admiral Cockburn himself coveted an elegant coach he saw and ordered it hauled aboard his vessel.

Elsewhere his marines proceeded to do more plundering and burning, an exercise the Maryland Assembly in a resolution of May 28 viewed with "horror and disgust." He landed 3,000 men on Kent Island, which he used for a time as a staging ground. At the beginning of June another British fleet sailed in. The combined forces scattered over both the Eastern and the Western shores, marauding at will.

The next spring Cockburn zestfully took up where he'd left off. The American satirist James Kirke Paulding described him in "The Lay of the Scottish Fiddle" in 1814:

> Childe Cockburn carried in his hand
> A rocket and a burning brand,
> And waving o'er his august head
> The red-cross standard proudly spread,
> Whence hung by silken tassel fair
> A bloody scalp of human hair.

That summer the British forces in the bay were further augmented, for Napoleon's abdication in April 1814 had freed thousands of British soldiers and sailors to chastise the upstart Americans. The new troops were commanded by Gen. Robert Ross, a bright, blue-eyed Irishman who had distinguished himself in the Peninsular War. Ross and Cockburn got together in mid-August. One day shortly after they first met they stepped off Cockburn's ship to reconnoiter at the mouth of the Potomac. They talked about Washington, that inviting city. Cockburn was convinced that they could easily attack it, and Ross found his conviction contagious.

The battle plan the British command developed was classic both in conception and execution. A British frigate was sent up the Chesapeake past Baltimore to create a diversion in that direction. Two more frigates were sent up the Potomac to bombard Fort Washington, below Alexandria. Ross's troops were ordered to march north through Prince Georges County, to feint toward Washington as if they aimed to assault it from the southeast, and then to take the long way around and attack it from the northeast instead.

His men began their campaign by disembarking on August 19 at the village of Benedict on the lower Patuxent. Among them was the best observer we have, British or American, of the events of the next few weeks, a perceptive subaltern named George Robert Gleig. He kept a journal which he revised and published some years after the event, just as William Eddis did his letters.

Though the *Journal* wins no prizes for impartiality—Gleig is quite capable of remarking that "the low cunning which forms a leading part of the American character has long been proverbial"—it's full of close observation. He takes us with the British troops from Benedict all the way to Washington and then to Baltimore. The men make a variegated march through deep woods and what Gleig calls "wild savannahs," through fertile fields and tiny towns, through cool shade and torrid August sun.

The march toward Nottingham, the first town on the way, starts on the afternoon of the 20th in good order. For hours the troops don't see an American skirmisher. But the sun comes close to overpowering them; a third of the soldiers drop by the wayside, a higher proportion than Gleig has ever seen. After a night of bivouac and rest they take up the march again, this time through forests which give them shade but also give cover to American riflemen. When they reach Nottingham they find that it's just been deserted, for there's even bread left baking in the oven.

The next morning they advance toward Upper Marlboro, over a solid road and still in forest shade. Here and there they glimpse an American horseman and the rear guard, apparently, of a column of infantry. They camp overnight in Upper Marlboro and early in the afternoon of the 23rd take the road to Washington, this time in the face of some rifle fire. With the bulk of the troops Ross then makes a feint toward Alexandria.

The next day is historic for the British. The troops begin their march around the District of Columbia in line with the plan to attack it from the northeast instead of the southeast. Their immediate destination is the town of Bladensburg, which has the only bridge across the Potomac's eastern branch, the river we now call the Anacostia, and which must be crossed to get into Washington. Although the road dwindles to a bypath it's cool under the arching trees. Then the road widens; the country opens up. The sun hits the British with renewed force. The dust rises beneath their feet "in thick masses" and Gleig suffers the discomforts of the damned.

At noon a sudden turn of the road brings them in sight of Bladensburg. Just beyond the town the road leads to the little bridge. For the first time during the campaign the British see a formidable sight: three long lines of American troops drawn up on the brow of a hill on the far side of the river, as well as riflemen among the willows and larches on the bank. Though his men are bone-weary, Ross gives the order to charge to his light brigade. When they reach the bridge the American artillery, some of which has already opened up, blasts into them. "The riflemen likewise now galled us from the wooded bank with a running fire of musketry," Gleig says, "and it was not without trampling upon many of their dead and dying comrades that the light brigade established itself on the opposite side of the stream." [1]

1. [George Robert Gleig], *A Narrative of the Campaigns of the British Army at Washington and New Orleans* (London: J. Murray [1826, 2nd ed.]), p. 118.

After a determined attack from the decimated British the first line of Americans flees "in the greatest confusion." But not the second. The Americans can still sting. The battle goes back and forth, with the British light brigade overextended and the rallying Americans using their muskets as manfully as they had at Lexington and Concord. But the disciplined British troops move ahead. By the time their second brigade crosses the bridge they're threatening to surround the Americans. Then, says Gleig, the Americans "lost all order and dispersed, leaving clouds of riflemen to cover their retreat, and hastened to conceal themselves in the woods"—an action which he clearly considers reprehensible.[2] By four in the afternoon the rout is total, though Gleig concedes that the British have lost more men than the Americans: nearly 500 killed or wounded. The way to Washington lies open.

Ross has a third brigade in reserve and he orders it to march toward Washington at once while his first two brigades rest. It enters the city with almost no opposition. That night the brigade spends busy hours destroying government property including, Gleig says, "the Senate house, the President's palace, an extensive dockyard and arsenal, barracks for two or three thousand men, several large storehouses filled with naval and military stores, some hundreds of cannon of different descriptions, and nearly 20,000 stand of small arms." [3] For the citizens of Washington it's "a night of terror." They flee in confusion. The streets are "crowded with soldiers and senators, men, women and children, horses, carriages, and carts loaded with household furniture, all hastening toward a wooden bridge which crosses the Potomac." [4] Throughout the city the flames rise so high that Ross's remaining men, now trudging on to Washington, can see one another's faces in the "dark red light . . . thrown upon the road."

The glow of the fires could be seen even farther away. It could be seen in Baltimore.

But the people of Baltimore were neck-deep in their own troubles. Scharf quoted an impassioned if unidentified writer:

2. [Gleig], *Narrative*, p. 120.
3. [Gleig], *Narrative*, p. 126.
4. [Gleig], *Narrative*, p. 131.

"The prospect to which they looked forward was indeed gloomy—to the sailor, imprisonment and fetters; to the soldier-citizen, the prison-ship; to the merchant, confiscation and ruin; to the house-owner, the torch of the incendiary; and to the chaste matron and her pure and beautiful daughters, the foul license of a brutal soldiery." [5] Luckily the brutal British soldiers, assisted by the brutal British sailors and marines, were either regrouping or plundering elsewhere. For plundering, Alexandria in particular was a nearer and easier target. Acting in reality with all the politeness war permitted, the British left Alexandria undamaged in return for, according to Walter Lord's *Dawn's Early Light,* 13,786 barrels of flour, 757 hogsheads of tobacco, "and countless tons of cotton, tar, beef, and sugar."

The British commanders were divided about what to do next. Should they devastate Baltimore at once or avoid the heated humors of the Chesapeake in summer and devastate farther north? Say in Rhode Island? Swayed by Cockburn's urging they finally decided to give priority to Baltimore, rich and truculent town that it was.

They didn't make the decision till September 7, thereby donating to Baltimore nearly two golden weeks to prepare defenses. The double disaster of Bladensburg and Washington had galvanized the city. In this time of crisis the heads of the armed forces and the citizenry united to pick leathery Sam Smith to lead them. A veteran soldier-politician, still gifted with driving energy, he ranked as the commanding general of the Third Division of Maryland militia. In the last week of August he took over like a cyclone. He swept together the remnants of the Maryland militia left after Bladensburg. He ordered the citizens out, with their shovels, picks, and wheelbarrows, to start digging on Hampstead Hill to fortify the eastern approaches to the city, where the British were expected. He welcomed the aid of militia from neighboring states and helped to get them equipped for battle. He wangled a $100,000 bank loan to buy supplies, for even ammunition was lacking. As the earthworks went up so did the number of soldiers to man them. In a week's time Sam

Smith had assembled under him six other generals and their commands. He directed them with the precision of a military bandmaster.

The British fleet anchored between Sparrows Point and North Point. Ross disembarked his troops and started, early in the morning of September 12, to march them north and then west toward the city. Cockburn ordered his ships up the Patapsco, toward the city likewise. At noon Ross requisitioned a lunch at the farm of one Robert Gorsuch. Afterward Gorsuch asked if he should prepare a supper as well. Loftily Ross replied, according to legend, that he would either eat in Baltimore that night or in hell. Before midafternoon he was dead, killed by a bullet from an American militiaman. He'd been riding alone when shot but the news of his death spread fast, disheartening his troops, for he'd been a charismatic leader. Notwithstanding, they rallied under his second-in-command, Col. Arthur Brooke. There was a brief but bloody fight near Bread and Cheese Creek and then in the face of a British charge the Americans gave way. Yet at least for a time they'd stood up to veterans of the Napoleonic Wars.

The next day Brooke's troops resumed their push. By mid-morning they were less than four miles from Baltimore. However, between them and the city rose Hampstead Hill. On it were new earthworks, crude but effective; ditches and trenches; and lines of poles hammered into the ground. American troops were everywhere; the hill swarmed with them, as the British command could see. Brooke probed, to find out if he could detour around the earthworks stretched across the hill. He couldn't; the Americans were protecting their flanks with more masses of soldiers. He and Cockburn decided to wait till the middle of the night to attack. However, Brooke had nothing like Ross's audacity, so he called a council of his officers to determine whether he'd made the right decision. No doubt out of a multiplicity of motives they urged him to retreat. Although Cockburn was outraged, there was nothing he could do about it. Brooke issued his orders and, at about the time the British troops had originally been told to attack, they turned around in a heavy rain and retreated to their ships. Subaltern Gleig remarked, mindful of the earthworks and the multitude waiting behind them, that a British "success under existing circumstances was, to say the least of it, doubtful." He added philosophically that even if the British had succeeded, nothing would have been gained.

Back at the British fleet orders went out for an advance up the Patapsco to batter star-shaped Fort McHenry, the city's key defense against naval assault. In its sixteen vessels the fleet included a rocket ship and several bomb-kedges with such alarming names as *Devastation, Terror,* and *Volcano.* Between six and seven on the morning of September 13 the assault began. It lasted for nearly twenty-four hours; the sight was both horrifying and, especially at night, spectacular. Each bombshell, weighing more than 200 pounds, had a fuse inside and was designed to go off on landing, scattering its lethal fragments. Often, though, the bomb detonated in midair. The rockets, much smaller and simpler, were designed to explode on impact but weren't particularly spectacular. However, the fleet also used signal rockets, which traced glaring arcs across the night sky.

An American commodore, John Rodgers, estimated afterward that between 1,800 and 2,000 bombshells were sent up and between 700 and 800 rockets. They did heavy damage to Fort McHenry but not heavy enough to make it surrender. Baltimore continued to look formidable. Slowly, grudgingly, the British fleet began to back off. The American forces could hardly realize it, and it wasn't till the 16th that Baltimore recognized that it had staved off the British on sea as well as land.

A contemporary ditty, "The Battle of Baltimore," summed it up:

> And Ross, Cockburn, and Cochran too,
>   And many a bloody villain more,
> Swore with their bloody savage crew
>   That they would plunder Baltimore.
>
>   .   .   .   .
>
> A day and night they tried their might
>   But found their bombs did not prevail,
> And seeing their army put to flight,
>   They weighed their anchor and made sail.

If we had to depend on those verses, Baltimore's ordeal probably wouldn't be remembered outside the state of Maryland. But happily there were other verses which have immortalized it. Francis Scott Key composed them, of course. First headed "Defense of Fort McHenry," a title with no tingle at all, they soon became "The Star-Spangled Banner." The details about the composition vary but the essentials are straightforward enough. Attorney Key boarded the British flagship to try to arrange the release of an American civilian, Dr. William Beanes of Upper Marlboro. He succeeded but the British, afraid to let him return because he might give away information about the bombardment they planned, put him on a packet off Sparrows Point. On its deck he watched through the day and night of the actual bombarding. Peering through a spyglass he saw by the dawn's early light, as he put it, that the American flag still waved over the fort.

Watching had been a torment to him, so his relief and enthusiasm were great. He scribbled a few lines and phrases on the back of a letter, added to them while the packet sailed into Baltimore, and produced a finished version in his hotel room that night. What he had composed was a rouser. Its rhythms were swinging anapests; its metrics as well as its melody were those of a popular British drinking song, "To Anacreon in Heaven." Its message was one of exultant patriotism, fit for a young country, our country. Our foes were haughty and boastful; they were also hirelings and slaves now consigned to their graves. We triumphed because God was on our side.

The sentiments and the era matched perfectly. Within a few months we possessed what we hadn't before: an anthem, stirring if unofficial, we could sing full-throated from then on. And it helped to convince us that we'd won the war.

Vignette: The Pageantry of Work

Work for many a man had more meaning a century and a half ago. The guilds and other work groups were a closer brotherhood than the labor unions of today. The fact showed in, among other things, their social bonds and their frequent public appearances. For instance, they relished taking part in parades. There were more of those then than now, and their pageantry was a lift to the spirit.

Witness the epic parade of July 4, 1828. The occasion was the laying of the first stone of the Baltimore & Ohio Railroad, at the point where it would enter Baltimore, by Charles Carroll, the sole surviving signer of the Declaration of Independence. The parade—marchers, riders, bands, floats—proceeded from the center of the city to the open field at the city limits where he ritually laid the stone; and then the procession returned. Ele Bowen describes it, group by group, in his *Rambles in the Path of the Steam-Horse* (1855). The result is a catalog, as a parade has to be, but a colorful one.

Old Sam Smith, still the hero of the Battle of Baltimore, had a place of honor in the parade; for he rode next to Charles Carroll in a landaulet and four. The guilds and working associations which followed them were led by the farmers and their floats. The first one featured a plow, two live mulberry trees complete with silkworms in their cocoons, and stalks of corn. The second featured a seedsman wearing epaulets of timothy grass and wheat. He had a bag of grain hanging from his shoulders and tossed out handfuls to the crowd as the parade progressed. After floats for harrowing, harvesting, and threshing, came the climactic one. It carried an apple tree with a grapevine on it and under the tree an actual cow was being milked. Over the cow fluttered a banner with the motto, "A land flowing with milk and honey," and near the cow was a pigpen with genuine, grunting pigs.

Among the other groups represented in the parade were the bakers, both loaf-bread and biscuit, dressed appropriately in white. The tailors' float carried a tailor shop with a master tailor and six journeymen. They were cutting and stitching a coat while the float moved along. They sported a banner showing Adam and Eve sewing fig leaves together. The painters' float carried a master painter at work on a portrait and a boy mixing colors for him. The cordwainers were making a pair of green morocco slippers for Charles Carroll as well as a pair of white satin lady's shoes. The hatters' float had a little hat factory along with two white hats, already made, for Charles Carroll and Sam Smith. The coachmakers were represented by an elegant barouche drawn by four gray horses, with postillions in blue livery. The metalworkers' float carried two coppersmiths making stills; two brass-founders, one making a pair of andirons and the other a set of stairrods; and two tinplaters, one making washbasins and the other tin tumblers which he threw out to the crowd as he finished them.

The fullness of the city and state's economic life was shown by the number of other groups in the procession. These were the gardeners; the millers and flour inspectors; the victuallers; the blacksmiths and whitesmiths; the weavers, bleachers, and dyers; the carpenters, planemakers, and lumber merchants; the stonecutters; the tool- and diemakers; the coopers; the printers; the saddlers and harnessmakers; the bookbinders; the watchmakers, jewelers, silversmiths, and engravers; the glasscutters; the ship-carpenters, ship joiners, and block- and pumpmakers; the boatbuilders; the ropemakers; the riggers, sailmakers, and pilots; the ship captains, mates, and seamen; and the draymen.

Of all these groups the draymen were the humblest—they marched at the end of the procession, in shirt sleeves, naturally—and the printers were the proudest. Their float carried an iron printing press fully attended, with owner, foreman, proofreader, compositor, two pressmen, and fly. The steward of the printers' chapel rode along as did two small boys dressed in flesh-colored tights and winged helmets as Mercuries. The Mercuries passed out copies of the Declaration of Independence and of an ode printed while the parade went on. The printers' proud motto was flaunted: "Printing, the Art Preservative of All Arts." And as a symbol of celebration their float carried half a hogshead of claret, labeled "summer ink."

3

Severn Teackle Wallis
and 19th-Century Life

8. Contentious Times in Baltimore

*N*OTEWORTHY among the July 1832 graduates of little Saint Marys College in Baltimore was a beak-nosed, weedy stripling named Severn Teackle Wallis. He bubbled with zest despite his slight appearance; his blue-gray eyes doubtless sparkled. Aching to be an author he decided to write his letter to the world. To begin with it would take the form of communications to the columns of the Baltimore newspapers.

Almost at once he was successful in getting his letters published, so successful that he soon started to save the clippings. He got a brown folio blankbook to paste them in; we can still leaf through it at the Peabody branch of Baltimore's Enoch Pratt Library. On the first page he penned a jingle confessing that the clippings were merely a start on his way to fame but that he was determined to achieve it by fair means or foul. The "fair means or foul" was youthful bravado; years later Scharf in his *History of Baltimore* dubbed him the "Sir Galahad of American barristers."

Long before the close of his career he achieved a full measure of fame. His name grew into a household word not only in Baltimore but throughout the state, and it was recognized in more

than one part of the nation. Today he's a nearly forgotten figure. In the recent and comprehensive *Maryland: A History* he
isn't mentioned in its 935 pages. Daniel Dulany the Elder,
though further from us by a century, remains the subject of historical research. Yet, despite manifold differences between the
two men, Wallis was almost as illuminating a figure for the
nineteenth century as Dulany was for the colonial era.

Both men became renowned lawyer-politicians; they had that
in common. But while property was close to an obsession with
Dulany it meant nothing to Wallis. Dulany owned lands so far-
flung that he could scarcely estimate their extent; Wallis died
without owning an acre. He maintained an old-fashioned office
in his modest home on Saint Paul Street and even when he led
the Maryland bar he charged small fees. Dulany divided his
time between the broad ranges of Prince Georges County and
the government's seat at Annapolis. He rarely visited the village
of Baltimore; he had scant reason to. But by the time Wallis
graduated, Baltimore—still a prime port despite the lingering effect of the British blockage, compounded by other adverse conditions—had become the focus of the state. It drew people and
energies from all over Maryland, from nearby states, and from
the far side of the Atlantic. Annapolis remained the capital, and
the rest of the state often banded together with it against Baltimore in resentment and envy; but Baltimore continued to en-
large its dimensions. For better or worse, by Wallis's time Baltimore was in many ways Maryland.

Politically Dulany was an insider, always close to power
whether he held office or not. Wallis relished nothing more than
the role of outsider. Several times he turned down offers of appointive office and he was a very reluctant candidate for elective
office. Yet he was no passive outsider, content to stand timidly
and watch. Throughout his career he fought with acerbic humor
and unflagging energy. Before the Civil War his most formidable foe was the American fascism of the Know-Nothing movement. After the war it was bossism as personified in the two
most cunning political managers in Maryland history, Freeman
Rasin and Arthur Gorman. Wallis was an uplifter, a reformer
who struggled to make people both better in character and better

off than they were, and freer politically. That meant all the people, beginning with the workingmen and their families. He even yearned to make the courts a citadel of justice. Dulany was a realist, with aims less lofty and far-reaching.

Dulany, we're told, spoke well both in the courts and in politics. But Wallis was celebrated as the most scintillating speaker of his time, especially when on the attack. His writing was equally effective. Dulany published only one pamphlet, though a classic one. Wallis poured out a stream of prose and poetry. He versified at will and wrote familiar essays with ease. With little trouble he published regularly in the Baltimore papers and occasionally in the magazines. What he wrote most often, and best, were the letters to the editor, argumentive pieces sauced with sarcasm, in which he tried to win the public to his point of view. Although both men loved learning and left libraries large for their time, Wallis was the greater scholar and wrote two books about Spain.

Personally they stood poles apart, in ways which had little to do with their eras. Dulany was tough and solid. Wallis was reedy and plagued with illness. How Dulany sounded when he spoke we can't be sure; but Wallis was famed for his high-pitched, precise, and fast-paced speech. Dulany was gregarious, a sociable and family man who married three times and lived surrounded by children. Wallis remained a finicky bachelor, attended for years only by a sister. Dulany valued friendship greatly, showing it to the extreme by his devotion to the rascally Macnemara and also, if less strikingly, by his cordial relations with many other, more respectable associates. Although Wallis asserted that he valued friendship much more than love between the sexes, his friends were few. His acquaintances were a multitude but that wasn't the same thing.

The Baltimore Wallis entered in the early 1830s was a turbulent one, plagued with problems more complex than Dulany had ever dreamed of. The economic depression of 1819–1822 which the state and nation endured was the worst so far. Baltimore particularly suffered because it was trying hard to industrialize but lacked both the capital and the banks to come up with the necessary credit. Bankruptcy and joblessness often threatened.

Nevertheless, the city kept its vitality and continued to be a lively place to stay in.

Wallis plunged into Baltimore life eagerly and published often from the summer of 1832 on. A born advocate, he couldn't take up his pen without taking sides. The clippings in his book, then and later, reflect his ready response to many of the events of this time, economic, political, and cultural.

The very first letter pasted in the book, dated October 1832, gives us a sign of things to come, in that it developed from his already-formed sympathy for the workingman of Baltimore. The sympathy was a bit surprising since his family had belonged to the Eastern Shore elite, and by graduating from college he had made himself the member of an additional elite. But it was genuine, as his career demonstrated.

The workingman's right to vote was being menaced by his employers, Wallis alleged in this letter, along with his very right to earn a living. "It has been declared by some employers that they will discharge every working man . . . who refuses to lay his rights at their feet and vote according to their dictation." Evidently they wanted that voting to be against the crusty Democrat, Andrew Jackson, who was campaigning for re-election as president; the clue in the letter lies in a kindly reference to Nicholas Biddle, head of the Bank of the United States and Jackson's aristocratic archfoe. Anyway, Wallis urged the workingman to assert his right to vote untrammeled and signed the letter "Free Suffrage."

As the months passed, Wallis recognized that the threat to the workingman's job, to his very livelihood, was formidable. After some better years the hard times of 1819–1822 had returned. Gradually they affected the employers directly as well as the employees. By late March 1834 Wallis was writing to the *Baltimore Chronicle,* "Never, in the times of our most gloomy prospects, did I behold ruin stare us in the face as it does at this juncture." He was right. The city was increasingly caught in the traumatic contest, both economic and political, between Jackson and Biddle; and the sympathy Wallis had for Jackson was being worn away. The immediate cause of the depression, to Wallis, was Jackson's obstinacy: "Firmness is a hero's virtue" but not stubbornness. "Look forth upon our streets," Wallis demanded; "Instead of the gay countenance and rapid step that mark the prosperous man of business, we behold the careworn visage and the sunken eye of groups that gather round the closed doors of a broken bank or ruined merchant."

For Baltimore the crucial blow was the suspension of business by the Bank of Maryland three days before Wallis penned his letter of March 27. The bank had been one of the most respected in the state. Its paper currency had been widely circulated; its deposits had been heavy; and its loans had run to the hundreds of thousands of dollars. Now it came crashing down. Like most Baltimoreans, Wallis thought that the reason was Jackson's withdrawing of public funds from the Bank of the United States the previous autumn and the withdrawing in turn by that bank of its funds on deposit at the Bank of Maryland. But rumors began to spread around the city that the men who ran the Bank of Maryland bore part of the blame. They were accused of manipulating the bank's stock for their profit, using the bank's deposits illegally, and taking kickbacks.

Three of the men involved were pillars of the state establishment. They were Evan Poultney, the ambitious president of the bank, and two of the bank's directors and counsels, the lawyer-politician Reverdy Johnson and John Glenn, a specialist in business law. Another bank, the Union Bank, was assigned the task of picking up the pieces of the Bank of Maryland. However, a rumor developed that Thomas Ellicott, the hulking head of his family's lucrative flour-milling business and of the Union Bank, had made a neat $25,000 through a shady deal with the Bank of Maryland.

Checking the rumors against some inside information he had, Wallis concluded that some of the rumors were all too accurate. He sent a letter, columns long, in June 1834 to the *Chronicle;* it summed up the case against Ellicott, a case which Ellicott disputed with all the guile at his disposal. But Wallis had at him with verse as well as prose. In July he published a "heroic poem" which opens:

> The devil was making a thunder storm
> At his lightning forge below,

When he heard the voice of Bank Reform
Across his kingdom go.

Wallis has the devil visit the Union Bank and catch Ellicott in
the middle of his misdeeds:

That moment he saw a man go forth
With a roll of notes in his hand;
And 25,000 was on a box
Close by, where he saw him stand.

. . . .

Old Nick gave forth a loud, laughing yell
And seized him by the hair;
Before one minute Tom was in hell
Keeping "silent meeting" there.

Throughout the next year Wallis kept up his newspaper warfare, with the squirming Ellicott still his chief target. Wallis's
sharp criticism of self-serving bankers hit home, the more so
because it was evidently based on legal principles. It revealed
the careful law student, for he'd commenced reading law in the
office of William Wirt shortly after graduation. Wirt, an author,
orator, and ex-attorney general of the United States, had settled
in Baltimore in 1829 only to die in 1834. Brief though their
contact was, it meant a good deal not only to Wallis but to Wirt.
After Wirt's death Wallis was able to transfer his studies to John
Glenn's office. We can guess that Glenn gave him some of the
ammunition he used against Ellicott in particular and bankers in
general. We can also guess that his reading law with Glenn
inclined him to focus his fire on Ellicott instead of broadening it
to include the Bank of Maryland trio.

Urging rational remedies the neophyte lawyer signed his letters "Reason" or "Order." But anger over the bankers' misdeeds swelled throughout the city, and it was directed not only
at Ellicott but at Glenn and Reverdy Johnson. It triggered a
revival of mob violence which the city hadn't experienced for
more than twenty years. Scharf commented that "the public,
which had lost heavily both in deposits and on the bank's notes,
and [had] borne the losses with wonderful patience, grew to
believe the whole affair a gigantic swindle, and the excitement

reached such a point that it could no longer be controlled." [1] Add to that a city administration too timid to try controlling, and the ingredients for rioting were ready.

It set in on August 6, 1835, when a mob stoned the windows of Johnson's mansion. Tempers then cooled only to heat up again. Feckless Mayor Jesse Hunt couldn't bring himself to call on the military. Instead he enlisted some citizens, gave them armbands, and beseeched them to preserve the peace.

On Saturday night, always a favorite time for trouble, a large mob met in Monument Square, a favorite place for noisy gatherings, around the monument commemorating Baltimore's fighting off the British in September 1814. A gang of the most volatile members split away and headed for Glenn's house. It had been barricaded but they smashed the windows, repulsed some of the armbanded citizens, and battered down the front door. Scharf said that "everything in the house was shattered to pieces or thrown into the street." They even demolished part of the front wall before more armbanded citizens plus some footguards dispersed them. The day after the sacking of Glenn's residence the rioters returned to Johnson's. They pitched its contents, including his splendid legal library, into the street and made a bonfire of them.

On Monday Mayor Hunt threw up his hands and resigned rather than grapple with the mob. Gen. Sam Smith, now in his eighty-third year, was called from retirement to lead the resurrected forces of law and order; and they finally put the mob down.

In the Baltimore papers the mob was both defended and attacked, in arguments typical of the time. The defense was that the mob was really "the people" and "the people" could do no wrong. The attack, led by Wallis, was that the mob was a group which subverted freedom and turned itself into an enemy of the people. And those who inflamed the mob should be stopped despite their claims of free speech: free speech gave no license for inciting to riot. The sufferers from its effects had every right to complain. On August 21, in a long letter to the *Chronicle*,

1. Scharf, *History of Baltimore*, pp. 784–785.

Wallis scored those who expected the victims of the mob to admire the action "which has given their habitations to plunder and conflagration, and has cast their wives and children out, houseless and homeless, on an uncharitable world."

In his own view Wallis was for the people but not for the mob; brawling democracy made him wince. From the outset he was a potential anti-Jackson Whig waiting for the Whig party to be born—his pro-Jackson "Free Suffrage" letter to the workmen in October 1832 was a flash in the pan. His anti-Jackson leanings were strengthened by the fact that his early friends and mentors were for the most part enemies of Jackson. The year before he went to read law with Wirt, Wirt had been picked as the candidate for president by the National Anti-Masonic convention, meeting in Baltimore, only to be battered in the election by Jackson. Wallis eagerly joined the Whig party when it was organized in Maryland in spring 1834. He cast his first vote as a Whig and he remained a Whig, though never a slavish one, for twenty years. Without hesitation he put his pen to the service of the party. At the same time that he was pillorying Tom Ellicott he was indicting Andrew Jackson.

Signing himself "Vox Populi" in a letter to the *Chronicle* of September 12, 1834, he leveled charge after charge against Jackson: Jackson had destroyed sound banking, had injured the welfare of the people, had winked at fraud by his subordinates, and had seized power belonging to the legislative and judicial branches of our government. Wallis dressed this Whiggish attack in his fanciest invective. On October 24 in the *Chronicle* he exhorted the workingmen of Baltimore to thrash the Jacksonians in the city election and show that Baltimore could still be free. Then the workingmen would again be able to sleep soundly at night. He signed himself "One of You." On October 6 the Jacksonians were indeed thrashed and the workingmen could again sleep soundly at night. On October 9 he printed a triumphant letter in the *Chronicle* jeering at the Jacksonians and hymning the virtues of the Whig cause.

Though the Whigs went on to more successes they soon solidified into a machine, and machine politics failed to attract Wallis. His political enthusiasms proved to be selective. He shunned the beery goodfellowship with masses of voters, the traffic in votes, and the debasing of issues which he saw many Baltimore politicians engaging in. His aristocratic urge remained to do things for the workingman, not with him.

However, political activity for what he deemed a good cause lured him from the start. That he was especially drawn to reform movements he realized before he finished reading law. In this respect he shared in the quickening interest in reform throughout the nation, the interest in widening the franchise, improving public education, and making the government more responsive to an educated electorate. Although in Maryland the statewide political issues during the early 1830s developed out of the depression, by the middle 1830s the major issue was reform, particularly reform of Maryland's political process. For one thing, reform demanded reapportionment. In spite of hard times the population of Baltimore was soaring; so, though less dramatically, was that of the western counties. But small southern counties on both sides of the bay, like Calvert or Caroline, still sent the same number of delegates to Annapolis as Baltimore County or Frederick County with four or five times more voters in them.

Reform meant a call for more than reapportionment, however. It meant an end to the undemocratic election of state senators, who were picked by a kind of senatorial electoral college. And it meant an end to the assembly's power to choose the governor of the state.

After much political scuffling the assembly passed a law in March 1837 making the major changes which had been demanded. The governor was to be elected directly by the people; so were the state senators. The senate was to be reorganized on the basis of one senator for each county and for the city of Baltimore. The house of delegates was to be reapportioned in favor of the heavily populated counties, and the city of Baltimore was allowed as many delegates as the most heavily populated county. Though the Democrats benefited more than the Whigs, Wallis was delighted with the outcome.

Politics charged the Baltimore air, not only for devotees like Wallis but for the citizenry; it was not only the staple of news in the papers but the staple of discussion on the street. One reason lay in the fact that when, in the early 1830s, political parties began holding national conventions to name their nominees for president and vice-president, Baltimore was a favorite site. The Democrats held the first half-dozen of their quadrennial conventions in Baltimore, beginning with the one in 1832. It set the precedent for excitement and spectacle. Apparently dull moments were few. Scharf noted impassively in his *History of Baltimore* that during "the proceedings of the convention a panic occurred, and one or two men jumped from a window and were somewhat injured." [2]

The Whigs were slower to select Baltimore but in the 1840s and 1850s they met there several times. Their meetings were heady affairs also, beginning in 1840 with the National Convention of Whig Young Men. The party had already picked its nominee elsewhere the previous December, but this didn't deter the Young Men from grandly reaffirming the nomination in Baltimore in May. The nominee for president was William Henry Harrison, who projected an image during the campaign of frontier simplicity and plain good cheer, of cabins and cider. Scharf has told us in another of his books that on May 4 "the hotels, boarding houses, and many private houses of Baltimore were crammed from cellar to roof to accommodate" the Whig visitors.[3] The convention began with a fixture of that era, a political procession, but a procession unusual in its colorful extravagance. Led by a barouche holding the mayor and Daniel Webster himself, it included delegations from the various states, each with appropriate banners and trophies. When the procession reached the convention hall the spectacle continued with "flying banners, clashing cymbals, restive horses, pretty girls, whole-souled politicians, log cabins, and hard cider." [4] After being harangued by Webster and Henry Clay among others, the

2. Scharf, *History of Baltimore*, p. 120.

3. Scharf, *The Chronicles of Baltimore: Being a Complete History of "Baltimore Town" and Baltimore City from the Earliest Period to the Present Time* (Baltimore: Turnbull Brothers, 1874), p. 500.

4. Scharf, *Chronicles of Baltimore*, p. 501.

convention acclaimed the Whig candidates Harrison of Ohio and
John Tyler of Virginia.

Wallis "was very enthusiastic and ardent" on their behalf in
the campaign, he remembered years later when talking about it
with a young friend named Henry Goddard.[5] However, he was
direly disappointed on meeting the president-elect. Because
Wallis generally set stiff standards for personal conduct he grew
indignant when Harrison began telling dirty stories. He thought,
he complained to Goddard, that he'd been campaigning for a
Cincinnatus, a high-minded old soldier who would leave his
plow only to rescue his country. Instead Wallis found that he'd
"voted for a blackguard." However, his disillusionment didn't
come close to damping his zeal for politics nor his zest in wielding his pen.

Memoir: Eastern Shoremen and Born-again Christians

Though Teackle Wallis was Baltimore born and bred, his
parents came from Eastern Shore families, the Wallises of Kent
County and the Teackles of Talbot. His roots lay in the most remarkable region of Maryland.

Seldom have the accidents of geography been more influential. On the map the peninsula to which the Eastern Shore
belongs hangs like a bunch of grapes from the mainland, with
its stem partly in Cecil County and partly in Delaware. By land
the only way to reach it for three centuries was through the
stem. By water it was more accessible but not, practically
speaking, much more. The ancestors of some of the Shoremen
hailed from the west coast of England, and they brought with
them a water-based culture which their descendants not only
preserved but, in their isolation, added to. Thanks to geography
their values and customs stayed substantially the same while
those of Baltimore altered steadily during Wallis's lifetime
under the pressure of tens of thousands of newcomers and the
growing pains of industrialism.

5. Henry Goddard, "Some Distinguished Marylanders I have Known," *Maryland
Historical Magazine* 4 (1909): 26.

Their mores reflected their isolation. Where communication was concerned, theirs was an oral rather than a written culture. They kept much of the idiom of their ancestors and as time passed they added expressions of their own devising. When Shoremen talk today, we doubtless hear echoes of antebellum words and phrases. In his book, *The Oystermen of the Chesapeake* (1970), Robert de Gast has brought together some examples of this speech, among them "neither" in the sense of "no"—"A man wants to follow the water, ain't neither way to keep him ashore." And "Honey" as a noun of man-to-man address. Shoremen storytellers still pass on the tales of haunted ships, stout folk heroes, and cunning rascals which came over from England with the first watermen. The ballads they recite or sing like "Sir Patrick Spens" or "Lord Randall" are ancient. Not that this isn't true for other parts of Maryland but it's more true on the Eastern Shore. And not that there aren't continual additions. In *A Faraway Time and Place: Lore of the Eastern Shore* (1971) a leading folklorist, George Carey, has printed not only old tales but such newer ones as those about an early twentieth-century strong man, gigantic "Lickin' Bill Bradshaw" of Smith Island. And in his *Maryland Folklore and Folklife* (1970) Carey has added new ballads to the old.

The Shoremen's actions were as independent as their speech. The most dramatic evidence of it is that between 1776 and 1851 they tried five times either to secede or to establish their right to secede under the Maryland constitution. James Mullikin has given us the story.[1] Even in colonial days the shore had its own little bureaucracy paralleling the Western Shore's. Each shore had a surveyor general; each had a provincial treasurer. This kind of equality survived the American Revolution, though the Eastern Shore had been totally Tory, and the forming of the new country. In 1809 the assembly created what came to be called the "Eastern Shore Compact." By its terms one of the two United States senators always had to be from the Eastern Shore. Notwithstanding, the shore remained restive.

1. In his chapter, "The Separatist Movement and Related Problems 1776–1851," in Charles Clark's *The Eastern Shore of Maryland and Virginia* (New York: Lewis Historical Publishing Co., 1950).

Sporadically it flirted with the state of Delaware, feeling closer to it than to Maryland. In February 1833 the governor of Delaware sent the governor of Maryland a set of resolutions passed by the Delaware House and Senate; these proposed that the two states negotiate a peaceful transfer of the shore to Delaware. The Western Shore's responses ranged from amusement to outrage, spiced by a feeling of "good riddance." In Baltimore the *American* of February 11 sniffed that it would be more logical for Delaware to join herself to the great state of Maryland. The resolutions reached the floor in March. They lost in the house of delegates twenty-four to forty; in the senate they lost by a single vote.

The Shoremen had their reasons for trying again. Looking across the bay at Baltimore, they saw a teeming, hostile city. The tide of reform sweeping across the country had reached the Western Shore. In Maryland it manifested itself especially in the call for reapportionment, which would give Baltimore far more power, and for the popular election of the governor. When the state accepted those and related proposals, the Shoremen feared that they would become the subjects of Baltimore. To them the reform movement which commanded the support of Wallis and his associates appeared a menace.

At best the Shoremen thought of themselves as stepchildren. During the two decades of public improvements in Maryland prior to the Delaware resolutions, the needs of the Shoremen were ignored. The state poured money into building the National Pike, a project which benefited Baltimore and western Maryland. It put money into the Chesapeake & Ohio canal project; the canal was designed to extend from Georgetown, next to Washington, west to Cumberland. It put money into the Baltimore & Ohio Railroad, so that it could stretch westward from Baltimore. All this benefited the Shoremen not a bit.

Obviously some appeasement was in order, if the political process was to work. In 1834 the assembly passed a bill giving the canal and the railroad $3 million each but also giving the Eastern Shore $1 million for its own railroad. It was to run the length of Maryland's part of the peninsula, connecting it at or near Elkton with railways to Baltimore and Philadelphia. The Eastern Shore smiled but not for long. The onset of the depression of 1837–1839 first hindered and then halted work on the road. As a matter of fact the shore never got it; when rail transportation finally arrived it was through spur lines from the Delaware railroad. Understandably, the shore agitated for separation several more times by 1851. Each time it was defeated and after the effort of 1851 it made no further political attempts of any magnitude. That isn't to say that the Shoremen felt less insular, less suspicious of Baltimore and the rest of the state. But they went about their daily work as usual.

We can see something of the daily work of the early nineteenth-century Shoremen in a quaint book by the Reverend Adam Wallace of Princess Anne, published in 1861. It's *The Parson of the Islands,* a biography of Joshua Thomas (1776–1853); the islands involved are Deal, Smith, and Tangier. We're shown how he and the other islanders got their food and livelihood from Chesapeake Bay, supplemented by some hunting. They couldn't live by agriculture on their marshy islands or on the fringes of the mainland. All they could hope to have were some patches of sweet potatoes or Indian corn, along with a few fields of wheat. Inland the fields of corn and wheat could be both large and luxuriant. Further, the soil was fertile enough—Sassafras loam in the north and Norfolk sands in the south—to promise well for truck gardening. But that was inland, and anyway few Shoremen cared for a life of hoeing weeds.

A cheerful youngster despite his family's grinding poverty, Joshua grew up in Potato Neck in windy Somerset County, where kind neighbors taught him the skills of fishing, tonging, and hunting which his stepfather was too besotted to teach. They taught him to paddle and sail the log canoes, hollowed out of pine, which were the Shoremen's most familiar means of transportation. They taught him to sail their small, two-masted schooners called pungies. And then with a natural envy they observed his fisherman's and hunter's good luck. He firmly credited it to the religious feelings he'd had since childhood. He found fish because, he said, "I was in the habit of praying to God, to direct me where the fish might be found." [2] After finding them he never forgot to kneel in his canoe and praise God. When he went hunting he found fowl, probably the ducks and geese coming from Canada to winter in the bay area, for the same reason. After bringing his birds down, he regularly knelt in the muddy marshes and praised God again.

No market to speak of existed for the fish Joshua and his neighbors caught during the decades before the Civil War. They ate what they landed. However, a thriving market for oysters developed in Baltimore and beyond. Though it's an exaggeration to call the bay one great oyster bed, it's a fact that it yielded a rich harvest in antebellum days and for a time afterward the richest harvest in the world. In 1839 the oysters the Shoremen got from the natural oyster beds, which they called "the rocks," amounted to 710,000 bushels. In 1850 the harvest was 1,350,000 bushels and in 1858–1859 3,500,000 bushels. [3] The American oyster in the Chesapeake, *Crassotrea virginica*, was a bonanza.

In Joshua Thomas's day the Shoremen still preferred tonging in shallow waters, of which there were many along the shore. The tongs were a pair of iron rakes on long wooden handles; they worked like scissors. The Shoremen also had smaller tongs called nippers, which they could use in shallower water still. The big tongs could scrape up a peck of oysters at a time from the bay's bottom. The Shoremen used their log canoes to go tonging but when they went out into deeper water, say fifteen feet or over, they sailed in pungies and used dredges. Wallace describes these as "large iron bags, formed of a kind of chain work, with a firm open mouth, the bottom part of which is a kind of rake." [4] They slung a dredge on each side of their pungy, then hauled the dredges up periodically as the vessel

2. Adam Wallace, *The Parson of the Islands: A Biography of the Rev. Joshua Thomas* (Philadelphia: Methodist Home Journal, 1870 edition), p. 57.

3. Caswell Grave, *Notes on the History of the Oyster in Maryland and the Physical Valuation of Her Oyster Properties* [Baltimore?: 1912?], p. 3.

4. Wallace, *Parson*, p. 42.

sailed back and forth, and scooped up oysters not by the peck but by the bushel.

Dredging ("drudging" to the Shoremen) was forced on them through the competition of Yankee fishing fleets. Having destroyed the Cape Cod oyster beds early in the century through overdredging, they sailed south to the Chesapeake. When crabbing began commercially, in midcentury, the greedy Yankee fleets sailed south for that too.

The Shoremen also went crabbing, especially for the succulent blue crab, *Callinectes sapidus*. Although for long years they apparently ate more than they sold, after the Civil War they saw the blue crab rank second only to the oyster in its commercial importance. They searched both for the mature males, called "Jimmies," and the mature females, called "sooks"— both being terms of unknown origin. The trotlining they practiced came from England. They paid out long lines tied every ten feet with bait, often bits of eel. They anchored one end of the line and then slowly hauled in the other to their boat. When eeling they used an eel gig, like a Neptune's trident except that it customarily had five prongs. The eel pots which they dropped to the bottom were woven with willow strips as, once again, they had been on the west coast of England.

As soon as Joshua was old enough he hired out to a neighbor as a waterman. A sturdy young fellow and a typical Shoreman, he looked more at home on water than on land. Like his mates he rarely wore boots and he kept his trousers rolled. A minister seeing him one Sunday reported that he wore "a little round hat, a light striped jacket, pants rolled half-way to his knees, and his shoes under his arm." [5] Typically again, he married early and soon had a family. However, in one way he differed, from boyhood on, from his neighbors and that was in the depth of his religious feeling. Because the established Anglican church seemed stolid to him, he turned to a livelier faith, Methodism. On the Eastern Shore in the early nineteenth century, Wallace wrote enthusiastically: "The Methodists were gaining

5. Wallace, *Parson*, p. 68.

ground very fast. Great revivals had swept through Accomac
and many parts of Somerset. Camp meetings had been started
and produced a wonderful effect on the popular mind and heart.
The people would crowd to the meetings, full of prejudice, fall
under the word, and start into new life.'' [6]

At a camp meeting in Annemessex, Joshua Thomas was born
again. One night he wandered in restlessly and listened to the
sermon. As he heard the preacher's exhortation, it came to him
that he was about to belong to the Lord. He "felt a gracious
change" run through his whole being and became so filled with
the spirit that he "could not help shouting to the glory of God."

From then on, simple waterman though he stayed, he determined to preach the gospel of Methodism. He joined the expanding Methodist church, first being made a licensed exhorter,
then a local preacher, then a deacon, and last an elder. Though
ordinarily he stammered, his religious zeal made an eloquent,
persuasive preacher out of him. For the Shoremen he became
their best-loved evangelist. He sailed everywhere around the
islands in his log canoe, which he named the *Methodist,* and
preached whenever he could. They called him the "shouting
preacher" because he punctuated his sermons with stentorian
calls of "Glory." And he not only shouted, he leaped. Just
prior to one sermon he exclaimed, "It comes to me, I must first
shout!" Then he began to jump and clap his hands, crying
"Glory, Glory . . . until he was in a fine glow of religious fer-
vor." [7] When some of his more sedate colleagues raised an
eyebrow he said stoutly that he regarded shouting and leaping as
means of grace.

Brother Thomas proved to be at his peak in camp meetings.
A notable one took place in summer 1838 at Deal Island. The
campgrounds were used every summer, so they had a circle of
permanent tents, made of weatherboard and shingles, as well as
temporary canvas tents. Nearby stood dining rooms and a meeting ground for black Methodists. An engraving in Wallace's
book pictures the whites' camp, with its rows of crowded

6. Wallace, *Parson,* p. 71.
7. Wallace, *Parson,* p. 222.

MARYLAND

A photographer's essay by Don Carl Steffen

Photographs in sequence

Farm in Frederick County.
Harvesting corn in Washington County.
Bloody Lane, Antietam Battlefield.
Surf fisherman, Assateague Island.
Oystermen, Chesapeake Bay.
Great Falls of the Potomac.
William Preston Lane, Jr., Memorial Bridge, Chesapeake Bay.
Sandy Point State Park and Lane Memorial Bridge.
Marble stoops, Baltimore.
Apartment buildings, Ocean City.
Downtown Cumberland.
Chesapeake and Ohio Canal, Potomac.
Annapolis harbor.
Downtown Baltimore.
Covered bridge near Frederick.

benches and with the exhorter on his small wooden platform. Brother Thomas preached just before a tremendous gale whipped through the island and then he gathered the scattered worshippers after it. Buffeted and dismayed, they were far from willing to listen at first. But he roused them with his inspiring words. As another minister noted with awe, "No man living will ever write the address which he delivered that day." [8]

On his death in autumn 1853, he was buried near a meeting ground at his request, mourned by Shoremen up and down the Bay. His influence has obviously lingered; no doubt partly because of it a good many of today's Shoremen are old-style Methodists. They still say grace before meals on the fishing boats and some of them have certainly been "born again."

9. Wallis: The Creative Mind: Writing, Speaking, Studying

Meanwhile, life in Baltimore went busily on. It covered more of course than politics or economics, more than garish conventions or brawls over banking.

For Wallis it included the cultural life of the time and the life of the mind. His interests both broadened and deepened. They broadened as his rising reputation as an author and orator brought him into contact with a growing number of cultural groups. They deepened as he continued his intensive study of the law and his rewarding researches into Spanish life.

This sounds a bit heavy but it doesn't take into account the zest he brought to whatever he did. He found life not only interesting but often amusing; he often wrote with his lips edged in an Augustan grin. The earliest letter dealing with his cultural concerns shows that. An unsuspecting correspondent of the *Baltimore American* suggested that the city needed a horticultural society. Though nothing could seem less controversial Wallis sallied out to demolish the idea. In a letter in November 1832 he asserted that the city didn't need such a society and shouldn't have it. Baltimoreans ought to relish the beauties of nature, not

8. Wallace, *Parson,* p. 242.

the blooms of hothouse flowers! If they yearned to study botany, Saint Marys College, "the pride of our state," already boasted a botanical garden second to none in America.

It developed that Wallis wanted a literary society instead. He wondered loftily in March 1833 "why there should be so little spirit among the young men, so little desire to encourage literary associations?" Another correspondent in the *American* pointed out that such groups already existed, among them the Young Men's Society. No, Wallis rejoined, that wouldn't do. The Young Men's Society was dedicated to moral improvement; what he wished was literary improvement through a society formed from "the elite of our youth" and dedicated to composing essays.

It was a tempest in a teacup but the town was full of such tempests as well as bigger ones. Anyway, young Baltimore shrugged and formed the botanical instead of the literary society. Undaunted, Wallis went ahead and produced literature by himself, poetry and prose both. Nearly always the poems proved to be standard-sentimental; often the essays were watered-down Washington Irving. Except for the wit. It salted much that Wallis wrote; and in his early prose it was often wit at the expense of some local grandee, wit giving us a view of Baltimore we don't usually get in the histories.

For the *Baltimore Visiter,* starting in July 1834, he composed a series of caricatures of resident dignitaries, starting with those at the bar. He gave his lawyers pseudonyms—"Mr. Rackrent," "Mr. Feeman"—but his contemporaries had no trouble identifying them. We do, however; though he scribbled down their names in the margin of his clipping book, he later scissored them out. This is the way he etches "Mr. Rackrent": "He is small and consequently aims at the magnificent. . . . When he rises word jumps out by word, as if an active carpenter were chipping in a dry block, and chip followed chip with the rapidity of lightning. As he grows warm with his subject, his head, arms, legs, and lips start off in a simultaneous jog-trot—his very whiskers are violent in gesture."

The next month he made fun of several of the city's prominent clergymen. Again he masked them with pseudonyms; again he identified them in the margin of the clipping book. This time he let the identifications stay. So we know that one of his prime targets was the rector of the leading Protestant church, William Wyatt of Saint Pauls Episcopal. Scharf once described the half-Grecian temple Wyatt presided over: "The portico was supported by four fluted marble columns, and the steeple was considered the handsomest in the United States." [1] Wallis himself passed periodically under that portico, for according to his grandniece Lucille Wallis he was a lifelong pewholder at Saint Pauls.

Wallis christens him the "Rev. Dr. High-Church" because Wyatt is devoted to religious ritual and has already quarreled publicly with his Unitarian neighbor, the historian-minister Jared Sparks, about his informal religion. Wallis paints Wyatt as imposing in appearance, elegant in manner, and highly attractive to the ladies. When he starts preaching a sermon he tries to be grave and majestic but, by the time he finishes, succeeds only in being affected and pathetic. Enjoying an ample salary from his prosperous congregation, he glides easily over the surface of life. He's a born "gentleman of the cloth" and Wallis predicts dryly that he'll be canonized someday. The "Rev. Mr. Quid" is quite the opposite. Wallis describes him for us, along with a cluster of other clergymen, in the *Visiter* in September 1834. A true Marylander, Quid is almost as dedicated to tobacco as to religion. In church he removes his plug from his underlip only when preaching or praying. "Quid" is John Mason Duncan, a maverick pastor of a maverick congregation that has seceded from the Presbyterian Church.

Next Wallis turns to medicos, starting with "Dr. Abraham Mortar-Scull," who never earned a medical diploma but waxes fat by cultivating the arts that please, among them playing with his patients' children and chatting with their mamas. He's really Dr. Solomon Birckhead, whom Wallis puns into "Brick-Head" and then into "Mortar-Scull." In October Wallis switches to businessmen and gives the readers of the *Visiter* "Mr. Tureen." He's actually a German immigrant named Schaeffer who has

1. Scharf, *History of Baltimore*, p. 520.

grown wealthy by manufacturing pots and pitchers. Now he's climbing clumsily up Baltimore's social ladder. "He subscribes to all the fashionable periodicals and encourages the Fine Arts," Wallis writes with a smirk.

Besides giving his readers a gallery of Baltimore mandarins he offers them some of his personal essays. They're scattered throughout the clipping book. Their style is elaborate but familiar, seeming to accost the reader and hold him by the lapel. Their tone is often playful, their mood sometimes nostalgic. Though Wallis is so young that he has little to be nostalgic about, he relishes adopting the persona of an old man. In November 1834 he begins a series for the *Visiter* called "Country Sketches," describing himself as an elderly retired lawyer, a bachelor who has left the noise of the city to "fly into Nature's arms." He now makes his home with an old uncle and aunt and enjoys it. The home is a pastoral plantation. Its fields are green; its air is soft; and its slaves are "fat and happy." The effect on him is profound. In a city church he would fall asleep; but in the country, given "the beauty of heaven and the silence of earth," he can sit and reflect with "unharnessed spirit."

Today hardly a newspaper prints poetry but in the days when the youthful Wallis was penning stanzas, editors thought they had a duty to promote American literature. He takes advantage of the fact to send out reams of verse. Their quality is betrayed by the first poem he pastes in the clipping book. Published in the *Visiter* in April 1834, it's a eulogy to William Wirt, who has just died. We can get the rather dreadful banality of it from a single passage about Wirt as an orator:

> His was the magic
> To strike the silver chords whose music vibrated
> Through the warm pulses of the feeling soul.

The only quality which raises his poetry above the flat average is an occasional touch of the same wit that glints in his prose; the same sense of the ridiculous that gives us his caricatures also gives us the doggerel about the devil and Tom Ellicott.

However, there's another serious poem, printed in the *Visiter* a month after the eulogy, that's worth a look because it reveals something deep in Wallis's personality. Entitled "Friendship and Love," it maintains that man's love for woman is burning, selfish, and soon sated. But friendship stands "beyond lust's boiling tide"; its joys are the joys of the mind, not the body. These aren't typical sentiments for a young man, not quite eighteen, but they're surely sincere. They're the sentiments of a young man given to acting the elderly bachelor, whose grandniece once remarked on his "inability to develop warm, close, personal relationships." [2] He goes to parties small and large but there's no sign that he partners many young women. He's more apt to play the odd man out. For instance, in 1837 Mrs. B. I. Cohen gives an elegant fancy-dress ball. Most of the guests wear colorful costumes; not Wallis—he goes as a mendicant monk.

The picture we get, then, is of a person who preferred the company of his peers. He relished the evenings with them when he wasn't immersed in his studies or his writing. Young lawyers and merchants for the most part, they evidently responded with affection and respect. Affection because he was a good companion, respect because the Baltimore bar had seldom known such a promising young attorney.

Partly through his eloquence in court, he quickly acquired his reputation as an orator. Today we value the conversational style of speech; other modes usually make us impatient. But in antebellum America skill with the spoken word was admired almost as an art form. Even in his old age Wallis kept the characteristics which combined to make him the most effective of Maryland orators. A Baltimore lawyer named Charles Morris Howard, a young fellow when he first heard Wallis, still remembered him years later. In a piece for a local paper he recreated the tall, thin man whose delivery was so rapid-fire that no shorthand reporter could take everything down and yet whose enunciation was so clear that you caught every syllable.[3] His body was alive with gestures which enriched his meaning.

2. Quoted in Sister Marie Haigley, "Severn Teackle Wallis: Protagonist of Reform," (Master's thesis, Catholic University, 1965), p. 11.

3. Charles Morris Howard, "Personal Recollections of Severn Teackle Wallis," *Baltimore Daily Record*, February 23, 1939.

His words were often tinged with irony, yet, wrote Howard, they never lost moral earnestness.

His reputation spread. Since he was also becoming known as an author, he began to be showered with invitations to speak before various societies, in nearby states as well as in Maryland. Not surprisingly he was at his best when addressing educated young men. One evidence of his rising star was the fact that half a dozen literary and philosophical societies elected him to honorary membership. Most but not all were made up of college students. Sometimes they requested a special lecture from him as well as the privilege of inscribing his name on their rolls. This kind of distinction began to be offered him in the early 1840s and continued for at least a decade. Among the societies electing him were the quaintly named Caloragathian Society of his own college in 1842; the Cliosophic Society of Princeton in 1843; the Goethean Literary Societies of Marshall College in the same year; the John Marshall Institute of Baltimore in 1844; and the Union Philosophical Society of Carlisle in the same year. Touched, Wallis saved all their ultra-polite letters; they still lie among his papers.

Somewhere in any history of Maryland there ought to be room for representing the life of the mind, not institutional but individual. For us Wallis may be the proper person to represent it. He was almost as brilliant a scholar as he was an advocate, and as hard-working.

His college experience was happy. In July 1833, like many a new alumnus, he went back eagerly for his first commencement after graduation. Then through a letter to the *American* he put in his usual good word for Saint Marys. "The youth of Maryland may now enjoy the advantages of an academical education," he asserted, "without wandering beyond the boundaries of their native state—the rich repast of literature is spread for them at home." He particularly praised the schooling in Spanish and French which the students could get. This was in part because the Sulpicians, the Catholic order which ran the college, kept close connections with the Continent. He didn't say this, though, since some anti-Catholic feeling existed in Baltimore.

Instead he urged his readers not to dislike the college because of its religious origins. Then, being Wallis, he went on, tongue in downy cheek, to decry the extreme youth of this year's graduates (he himself having graduated when not quite sixteen) and impudently signed the letter "Senex."

Spanish became his specialty. He began his study in college, where he was taught by Don José Antonio Pizarro. Because Baltimore ranked as an international port many countries stationed consular officers there, and Don José was Spain's vice-consul. He found the boyish Wallis a delight and shared with him not only his knowledge of Spain's language but also of its literature and life. Graduation strengthened their intimacy instead of weakening it and for many years Wallis paid a visit every day to his old professor. That he played a considerable part in the shaping of Wallis's mind is patent.

Wallis stayed almost as devoted to his old college as to Don José. He kept up his association with his other teachers and he received a master's degree there two years after graduation. As he grew more expert in law, he furnished the college with legal advice. For its part the college proudly watched his meteoric ascent. In summer 1841, only nine years after he graduated, it awarded him an honorary LL.D. degree and, inevitably, invited him to deliver the commencement address. It must have been a gratifying day.

His legal training was probably equally important in molding his mind. It began with the tutelage by William Wirt, who displayed an exceptional interest in his apprentice. We have a long, rich letter from Wirt in the summer of 1833.[4] He concentrates on what Wallis should read in order to improve his thinking and on how he should conduct himself. He took Wirt's advice seriously; for the authors Wirt recommends were found in Wallis's library on his death, and the conduct Wirt recommends was clearly evidenced in some of Wallis's actions.

"Have you dipped into the works of Edmund Burke?" Wirt begins. His speeches are splendid, his essays even better. He's a

4. Letter, William Wirt to Wallis, August 25, 1833; Wallis Collection, Peabody Department, Enoch Pratt Free Library. Used with permission of the Enoch Pratt Free Library.

masterly reasoner and a model for Wallis to follow. Wallis must draw from the dead as well as the living. When it comes to legal thinking he must widen his horizon, bring up his arguments from greater depths, and learn to fold his adversary in "coils of a more *anaconda* gripe." Other authors worth his study include John Locke and Francis Bacon.

Then comes a surprising bit of advice. For Wirt "the age of ornament" in address is over. Consequently, he lauds Daniel Webster for his "rough, abrupt strength" of speech and encourages Wallis to copy him. He concludes by advising Wallis to keep files of important newspapers the way Thomas Jefferson did, to keep a commonplace book of quotations, and to keep a diary. Wallis proceeded to do all these things.

He likewise listened with attention and learned fast from other leaders in the legal community. From John Glenn, of course, under whom he finished his legal training, but also from such a legal luminary as Reverdy Johnson, renowned for his skill in debate. The anonymous editor of the collected *Writings* of Wallis recalled him at this stage as "one of the favorite juniors and associates of the great leaders of the bar." [5]

With his gusto and abounding energy Wallis could apply his mind to the law without neglecting his study of Spain. In fact his standing as a scholar grew so high that in 1843, thanks in part no doubt to the good offices of Don José, he was elected a corresponding member of the prestigious Academy of History in Madrid. In 1847 he realized a cherished hope by visiting Spain. Searching for better health, he decided that a sea voyage to a softer climate would be an admirable idea. Naturally Spain lay at the end of the voyage; naturally he took his habits as a scholar and writer with him despite his uncertain health. The result was the publication by Harpers in 1849 of his first book, *Glimpses of Spain,* dedicated to Don José. The title is unpretentious; so is the subtitle, *Notes of an Unfinished Tour.* Yet the book quickly attracted attention. Far from being mere "glimpses"—the book runs to more than 400 pages in the collected

5. Severn Teackle Wallis, *Writings of Severn Teackle Wallis* (Baltimore: John Murphy, 1896), 1: xiii.

Writings—it's an extended survey of Spain as seen by a cultivated, sympathetic tourist. He wrote about everything from cathedrals to gypsies, from paintings to food. The book is still interesting reading though marred for us by a prissy tone.

Glimpses led to an ideal assignment which combined his training in law with his scholarship and then extended both. In Washington the federal government was casting around for someone to help it solve a vexing problem about Spanish lands in America, specifically, about who owned most of the eastern part of the Florida peninsula. The United States asserted that it did and so could deed the land to any of its citizens. Spain asserted that the Spanish duke of Alagon owned the land. Having heard of Wallis's reputation, the secretary of the interior, Thomas Ewing, commissioned him in September 1849 to return to Spain. His job was searching the archives in Madrid to find out what Spain's land-granting practices had been and whether the Florida grant conformed legally to those practices. Though we lack the details of his findings we can deduce that they favored the United States; for during the investigation the Spanish government tried to impede him and after the investigation the American government pronounced itself pleased by the results.

For himself he got another book out of his return to Spain, the knowledgable *Spain: Her Institutions, Politics, and Public Men.* Published in 1853 by Ticknor when Wallis was thirty-seven, it's a rambling survey running to 377 pages in the collected *Writings.* Its contents go beyond the scope of the title, for they include commentary—often still interesting—on lodging houses, dress, and everyday life in Madrid. He dedicated it to John Glenn, who was then crowning his life's work with a federal judgeship.

Wallis never lost his scholarly habit of mind nor his interest in institutions of learning. Throughout his career he continued to compose essays, addresses, and poems—not to mention letters to the editor. One index of his place in the city's developing intellectual life was that he was a founder and later a president of the Maryland Historical Society, a provost of the University of Maryland, a president of the board of trustees of the Peabody

Institute, and an influential friend of the Johns Hopkins University.

Memoir: Fuel and Fuelers

Much as in the twentieth century, there was the problem of energy as the nineteenth century advanced. Baltimore hungered for power in order to industrialize. The city lacked the abundant waterpower which the fall line provided for New England industrial towns. Something was needed beyond cordwood to heat the boilers whose steam would turn the wheels and shafts of industry. That something was fossil fuel. It was already known to exist in considerable quantity at the northwest corner of the state, in Allegany County.

George Washington himself, traveling through the region, suggested in 1755 that beneath its soil "the fuel of the future" might be found. Following him other travelers encountered beds of bituminous coal on the surface of the earth, and by the early nineteenth century a few small companies were tunneling into them. Made aware of the need for energy, the Maryland Assembly incorporated a dozen coal mining companies between 1828 and 1838. Their chief difficulty turned out to be not the mining of the coal but getting it to the users. To begin with it was floated down the Potomac on flatboats. In her lively book *Best-Dressed Miners* Katherine Harvey reported that coal worth six to eight cents a bushel in Cumberland brought fifty to sixty cents at the dock in Georgetown.[1] Though this water transport for coal promised well for mining companies and towns close to the Potomac, it didn't for Baltimore. Nor did the Chesapeake & Ohio canal, which was begun in 1828.

Salvation for the city lay in the Baltimore & Ohio Railroad, although the savior was a reluctant one, wanting guarantees and assurances before moving any coal an inch. The construction of the road had commenced the same year as the canal, at Baltimore's city limits. By November 1842 the road had reached Cumberland, 178 miles away. But the B. & O. management

---

1. Katherine Harvey, *The Best-Dressed Miners: Life and Labor in the Maryland Coal Region, 1835–1910* (Ithaca: Cornell University Press, 1969), p. 6.

was interested primarily in passenger traffic. It was both profitable and prestigious to move people fast. The management was
less interested in the humdrum business of hauling freight and
not at all interested in hauling bituminous coal. Coal was dirty
and moreover necessitated the building of freight cars which
could carry nothing else. Consequently the mining companies
had to guarantee to provide 175 tons a day in Cumberland 300
days a year. Then the B. & O. gave in.

Actually it took six years for the mines to provide that much
coal; not till 1847 did the tonnage level go over 52,500. But
after that it climbed remarkably, to almost 193,000 tons in 1850
and to 493,000 in 1860. Given good transportation, coal was
nothing less than black gold. Small wonder that money invested
in Maryland mining came from as far away as England. Surveys
disclosed that the supplies in the main bituminous basin in Allegany County were almost inexhaustible. It lay in Georges
Creek Valley between Dans Mountain and Big Savage Mountain, at its nearest point only eight miles from the railhead at
Cumberland. The so-called big vein was already famed for its
breadth and its thickness, estimated at fourteen feet. Also well
known were the Six-Foot Vein and the Four-Foot Vein. In
1854, according to Katherine Harvey, the total coal resources
throughout the basin were judged to be four billion tons.

Here was coal enough, once mining got well under way, to
give Baltimore all the steam power its growing factories
required; enough to keep Baltimoreans warm in winter, though
they preferred Pennsylvania anthracite to Allegany bituminous;
and enough to provide the gas for the city's multiplying
numbers of gas lights. The coal that Baltimore couldn't use
traveled to other Maryland towns and to East Coast industrial
markets north of Baltimore. The demand for it grew because the
coal was of high quality. Scharf in his *History of Western Maryland* quoted the navy's specialist in coal testing as having asserted in 1844 that "a pound of coal or bushel of coal from this
region will generate more steam than the same amount of coal
from any other mines in the country." [2] An equally convincing

2. Scharf, *History of Western Maryland: Being a History of Frederick, Montgomery,
Carroll, Washington, Allegany, and Garrett Counties* (Philadelphia: L. H. Everts,
1882), p. 1,316.

testimonial was that the B. & O. switched to Cumberland coal for its locomotives while some other roads were still burning cordwood.

And what of the men who mined the coal? Their life was hard, dirty, and dangerous, as Katherine Harvey showed. One of the earliest companies, George's Creek Coal & Iron, kept some of the most complete records; and they can enlighten us about mining life. For the company's miners it was lived in what became the company's town, Lonaconing, the ancestor of other company towns. Some of the miners came from Great Britain; so did some of the stockholders. A group of Baltimore and London capitalists set up the company in 1835 and soon recruited their foremen from the mining regions of Wales and Scotland. The recruiting continued till the Civil War and the foremen frequently brought relatives and friends to the mines with them.

They mined mostly by burrowing into the hillsides, putting up timber braces as they moved along and leaving pillars of coal to support the roof. But the bituminous coal was softer than anthracite and apt to crumble without warning. To get the coal the miners made horizontal and vertical cuts into the coal face with their picks. The horizontal ones were riskiest, for the miners had to lie on their sides to do the cutting. If coal collapsed above them, they could be crushed.

The wages which the miners received look miserable to us. All we can say for the George's Creek and other Maryland mining companies was that Pennsylvania and Virginia companies were worse. The Lonaconing miners were paid not by the day or hour but by the ton. Further, it was the long ton, 2,240 pounds. And the company did the weighing. In 1839 it set the miner's wage at 50 cents a ton, with the expectation that each miner would dig at least two tons a day. By 1850, with the coal industry burgeoning despite a bad year or two, the wage was down to 30 cents a ton. In 1854 it was down to 28 cents. Many miners struck at that point. However, when some of them staged what the *Baltimore Sun* termed a riotous demonstration, the company marshaled its private militia to control it and the sheriff afterward arrested the leaders, thereby breaking the strike.

The miners' houses were only log cabins in the first years at Lonaconing. After the company erected a lumber mill they improved. The specifications for one in 1845 called for a single-family house 32' x 32', 1½ storeys, weather-boarded outside, and with a roofed front porch. The outside was to be white-washed, the inside plastered and then painted. Some other houses were double; each of the two families living in them probably paid from $2 to $2.50 a month rent as of 1845. Many of the miners kept kitchen gardens, for Lonaconing soil was rich.

The company opened its school in March 1839 after a count showing sixty-four children of school age and ninety-four of preschool. The company's Episcopal minister served as school-master. The school operated till the Civil War. Because the company's inclination was Anglican, it turned down a petition in 1839 from twenty-five Presbyterians who yearned to build their own church instead of worshiping in the company one. However, the company compromised by letting the carpenters' shop be used on Sundays for Presbyterian services. The company church, called Saint Peters, was a long building with six-teen pews, capable of holding a congregation of a hundred to worship with the Episcopal minister.

The Welshmen among the miners were a close-knit group. Several Welsh lay preachers were in their number and they conducted Presbyterian services in both Welsh and English. The Welsh families brought along with them their love of singing and their hymns were enthusiastic and melodious. So were their other songs and, at the Eisteddfods they recreated, the singing echoed against Dans Mountain as it had against the Welsh hills.

The miners no doubt needed the consolations of religion, for not only was their labor arduous but their life was severely regulated. In 1839, when the town had 700 inhabitants, the company put forth the "Rules of the Lonaconing Residency." Once again, all we can say is that the rules in the Pennsylvania and Virginia company towns usually proved to be worse. For instance, they often forced the miners to buy at the company store by paying them in script or tokens redeemable only there.

The Lonaconing rules specified that every company employee in the town would work every day of the year except Sundays and Christmas day, from sunrise to sunset. The great bell of the company would toll at the beginning and end of work. Absence from work would bring either a loss in wages or discharge. No employee would be allowed to quarrel, gamble, or fire a gun. No employee could keep a dog without permission from the superintendent. An employee and his family, if he were fired, could be ejected from company housing by the superintendent "at any moment." Each employee would be paid once a month, in cash or by check, after deductions for debts at the company store, mills, and post office, and after a contribution to the medical and school fund. Remarkably enough, some Lonaconing miners had money left.

Half a year before the Civil War broke out, the journalist-poet William Cullen Bryant visited the Maryland coalfields to report on their conditions to the readers of the New York newspaper which he edited.[3]

He noted that it had been twenty-eight years since he'd glimpsed the valley of Georges Creek and it looked far different. Now there were iron-works: "smoking furnaces and forges and vast heaps of cinders." There were bustling villages. And above all there were coal mines. In his poetic prose Bryant described his party's approach to the entrance of one mine, "out of, which a train of loaded trucks was passing, every one of which was attended by a miner blackened from head to foot with the dust of his task, and wearing in the front a small crooked lamp to light his way." As the miners "emerged from the darkness," he commented, "they looked like sooty demons." The members of his party entered the mines fortified with guides and lanterns. They ventured into passages only partly propped with wooden posts. When they reached the coal face at the end of one passage, they found the miners driving wedges "into the cracks and fissures of the coal." They watched while several of the large blocks fell and the miners jumped aside.

A penalty of the miners' life was that it kept them ignorant—

---

3. William Cullen Bryant, letter from Mount Savage, *New York Evening Post,* October 22, 1860; quoted in Scharf's *History of Western Maryland,* pp. 1,436–1,437.

as Bryant phrased it, they owed ''little to the schoolmaster''—
and contemptuous of education. But Scharf, loyal as always,
added when quoting the remark in his *History of Western Maryland* that the current miners were intelligent men and that no
schools in the state ranked higher than ''those of the mining
regions of Allegany County.''

10. The Rise and Fall of Homegrown Fascism

All poor old William Henry Harrison did to make Wallis call
him a blackguard was to tell dirty stories. That was in 1841.
Only a few years later Wallis was confronted for the first time in
his political career with real blackguards, with primal political
evil. It came in the form of American fascism, though that term
hadn't been coined yet. It started in New York and Philadelphia
and then proceeded to Baltimore. In New York it developed an
ugly habit of violence; in Baltimore the habit grew uglier still.

In November 1844 a local Whig journal called the *Clipper*
proclaimed that it would hereafter support the ''American Republican'' party. In token of its commitment it changed its name
to the *American Republican* and wiped the arms of Maryland
from its masthead, setting a spread eagle in their place. Because
many a reader hardly realized that the party existed, the paper
enlightened them. This early in its life the party's program was
starkly simple: that only natives should be allowed to hold public office and that the naturalization of immigrants should be
allowed only after they'd lived here for twenty-one years.

The *Republican* touched a chord. Meetings in Baltimore and
western Maryland during the next months attracted crowds and
heard long debates about the proper planks to put in a regular
party platform. In March 1845 party members held a statewide
convention in Baltimore; in August, following the lead of the
fledgling national party, they altered their name to ''Native
Americans.'' Their leaders in Baltimore decided that the nearest
path to power lay in attracting the city's blue-collar workers
whose jobs were threatened by the immigrants. In September
the *New York Herald,* surveying the Baltimore scene, observed
waspishly, ''The Natives have had several mass meetings of late

and have succeeded in humbugging some two or three hundred mechanics, principally Democrats, into an adherence to their fanatical and corrupt schemes." [1]

The Native Americans put up a slate of candidates, mainly humbugged mechanics, for city and state offices in the October 1845 election, but they were roundly defeated. Nativism was an idea whose time plainly hadn't come. The party lost some of its members and others went underground, preferring to work in secret. On the surface the Whigs and the Democrats remained in control. But each year more foreigners came to the United States. They disembarked in New York and Baltimore as often as anywhere and gradually dominated the job market. And with the passing of each year the Whig and Democratic politicians became more embroiled in the slavery controversy and less attentive to the problems of immigration.

Both the Democrats and the Whigs held their nominating convention of 1852 in Baltimore; the slavery issue agitated both. After the Democrat, Franklin Pierce, beat the Whig, Winfield Scott, in the presidential race, the Whigs split badly. The Native Americans were now reappearing, with much more strength than before, and they beckoned to disgruntled Whigs to join them. With their new recruits the Nativists in Baltimore put up a full slate of municipal candidates in fall 1854, headed by one Sam Hinks for mayor, and after a heated campaign trounced the Democrats.

The Nativists' platform expanded. It became the banishing of all foreign influences in American life, the promotion of native American interests and ideals, and the correcting of political abuses in general and of voting irregularities in particular. That was the public platform. Beneath it, in the murky shadows, lay a private one whose emotional appeal grew for many a Marylander. It mingled hate, clannishness, and fear.

For its scapegoats, those objects of hatred which fascism seems to demand, the party seized on foreigners, especially the Irish and German immigrants, and the Catholic church, to which many of them belonged. Immigration from Catholic Ire-

---

1. *New York Herald,* September 23, 1845.

land had been climbing particularly because of the potato famine and from the Catholic parts of Germany for a variety of reasons, including hard times and military conscription. The non-Catholic Germans were often targets as well because they were suspected of being godless, though some of them were in fact church-going Lutherans. Hostility hardened toward the Catholic church; to suspicious Marylanders it looked like an alien power thrusting itself into American affairs. "No Popery" remained a useful political slogan.

As the party grew more potent its clannishness waned; however, it always kept a touch of the underground, an air of secrecy. Members acted as if they belonged to a brotherhood and in the early 1850s, significantly, two large Nativist lodges made their semipublic appearance, the "Sons of the Sires" and the "United Sons of America." Both established branches in Maryland. Members of the party itself were commanded, when queried in public about the party, to say that they knew nothing. Someone sarcastically dubbed them the "Know-Nothings" and the label stuck.

The fears which the resurgent Know-Nothings fed on were widespread and various. The workingman felt menaced, even more than he had a decade earlier, by immigrants hungry to displace him at a lower wage. The middle-class businessman, often a church-going Protestant, was repelled by the esoteric rituals and large claims of Catholicism. The upper-class leader, often bearing an old Maryland name, saw his control imperiled by a horde of naturalized voters.

But there was more to it than that. There was the image conjured up by the Know-Nothings of a return to old American standards of probity, simplicity, and purity—the standards supposedly of the ancient Roman Republic. It was an image associated with our good old days regardless of whether they ever existed. It was an image, the party leaders hoped, that summoned up the Spirit of 1776.

Almost from the start Wallis recognized the brute menace of the Know-Nothing movement. He even let himself be put up for office. In 1847, still a loyal Whig, he ran for the house of delegates; in 1851, still a Whig but an uneasy one, he ran for state's attorney in Baltimore. Both times he was beaten. Then he watched with deep concern while more and more Whigs gravitated to the Native Americans. Faced with the specter of a splintered party he decided to join the Democrats.

The Know-Nothings added victory in the statewide elections of 1855 to their victory in Baltimore with Sam Hinks the previous year. Having tasted blood, almost literally, they thirsted for fresh triumphs. When the new legislature met in Annapolis in January 1856, they controlled both houses. Their only effective opposition came from the holdover governor, a forthright Democrat named Watkins Ligon, and that wasn't much. They felt that they were equipped for a series of successes. Nothing was lacking. They had their platform; they had their scapegoats; they had their demagogues to rouse them; and they had their paramilitary forces.

The last is no exaggeration. From Baltimore's scruffiest streets came gangs of men who, flexing their biceps, gave themselves such names as "Plug Uglies" and "Blood Tubs." Baltimore had already known violence but nothing like what the Nativists unleashed. The result was the threat of mob force at all times and the certainty of mob rule at election times. In his *History of Baltimore* Scharf was as kind as could be, yet he felt obliged to give a whole chapter to "Mobs and Riots." And he showed that each Know-Nothing riot was worse than the one before.

He summed up the gory election of October 8, 1856: "In various parts of the city pitched battles raged all day; muskets and pistols were freely used, and even cannon brought out into the streets. Nightfall alone put a close to a scene more like the storming of a town than a peaceful election." [2] He added that by then the Know-Nothings had infiltrated the police department. Many of the constables who should have kept order stood indolently by. The newspapers reported that four men were killed and many more wounded. The presidential election, held the next month, proved even gorier. Ten men were killed and more than 250 were wounded.

2. Scharf, *History of Baltimore*, p. 787.

For the rest of the decade the elections were a shambles. Violence begot violence, and some of the Democratic clubs joined in the battling as did some of the fire companies. But the Calithumpians, the Eighth Ward Blackguards, the Butt Enders, and their Jacksonian kind were outgunned by the Plug Uglies, the Blood Tubs, and their street allies.

The shoemaker's awl and the blood tub became the Know-Nothings' pet devices. The awl was a handy weapon, easy to conceal and nicely adjusted to wounding without killing. By the end of the decade the clubs were waving banners with such warning slogans as "The Awl is Useful in the Hands of an Artist" and "Come up and Vote; There is Room for Awl." When the nativists' chief demagogue, a reactionary congressman named Henry Winter Davis, whipped up his hearers at a monster rally at the Battle Monument in October 1859, banners like that were displayed behind him on the speaker's stand; a three-foot awl dangled above his head; and in front of the stand a blacksmith at his forge turned out one awl after another for his audience.[3] Though more cumbersome, the tub proved nearly as effective as the awl. The practice was, again according to Scharf, to haul "to the polls tubs of blood from neighboring butchers' establishments; and whenever a luckless German or Irishman approached," to seize him, drag him to the tub, and squeeze a sponge full of blood over his head and face.[4] When let loose few voters did anything but run away.

At the polls the ballots were plainly marked by party; the Know-Nothings took to using striped paper for theirs. There was nothing private about the balloting. As a rule it was at an open window so that everyone could see which ballot was about to be cast. If a citizen carried a piece of striped paper in his hand he was allowed to vote. If he didn't the clubs intimidated or brutalized him.

The leaders of the Know-Nothing movement had other resources as well, among them what was called "cooping." It meant the shutting up of men, usually derelicts, in rooms or coops on election day and then dragging them from polling

3. Scharf, *History of Baltimore*, p. 787.
4. Scharf, *History of Baltimore*, p. 787.

place to polling place to cast their votes. To make them more docile while voting again and again, many of the men were drugged first or made drunk. Edgar Allan Poe was apparently cooped in the election of 1849 and died from the effects a day or two afterward.

Baltimoreans in the past had tolerated more than their share of reckless, even criminal, conduct. But they had no longing to live in a jungle, so during the second half of the 1850s opposition to the Know-Nothings mounted. Wallis stood at the center of it. Recognizing that the Know-Nothings had to be fought nationally as well as locally, he now worked hard for the Democratic party. In November 1856 the Democratic candidate, James Buchanan, won the presidency over Millard Fillmore of the Know-Nothing or American party and John C. Frémont, the first Republican candidate. Maryland was the single state that Fillmore carried. Soon after being sworn in, Buchanan offered Wallis the post of U.S. district attorney for Maryland. He declined. As an instinctive outsider he doubtless felt more comfortable if not in public office; perhaps he worried about his always delicate health. Perhaps too he was discovering like many another voter that he couldn't endorse the full platform of his party. For the Democratic party was being sundered, as the Whig party had been before it, on the rock of slavery. And as the American party was soon to be.

But in Baltimore the Know-Nothings saw small cause for apprehension. Writing from Annapolis one of their opponents, Judge John Legrand, exploded in helpless anger to his friend W. P. Preston on June 2, 1857: "I see by the papers of this morning that the Plug Uglies of Baltimore . . . have been going on in their usual murderous way. I wish that every wretch of them had met with a violent death." [5] In the city election of October they carried every ward but one. In the state election the next month their candidate for governor, stony-faced Thomas Hicks, carried Baltimore by nearly 10,000 votes. But only, as outgoing Governor Ligon said bitterly, through "outrage, violence, and organized ruffianism at the polls, whereby

5. Letter, John Legrand to William P. Preston, June 2, 1857; Preston Family Papers, Special Collection, University of Maryland Library. Used with permission.

multitudes of citizens, native and naturalized, were deterred from voting." [6]

During the steamy summer of 1858 a reform group began to gather. It issued a manifesto, probably penned by Wallis, who'd emerged as the most caustic public critic of the nativists. He'd found a forum through the older son of his mentor John Glenn. William Glenn was one of the proprietors of a Democratic paper called the *Daily Exchange* and he gave Wallis the freedom of the editorial page. Wallis used it with grim pleasure to excoriate the Nativists. The reform group rallied enough support to offer a candidate for mayor in the October 1858 election. They chose Col. A. P. Shutt, a political independent and, according to Scharf in his *History of Baltimore,* "a gentleman of integrity." But it was still too soon for integrity. The campaign was rougher than ever, with so much brutality that Shutt withdrew at noon on election day to protect the physical safety of his supporters. The Know-Nothing incumbent, Thomas Swann, ended with more than 24,000 votes and the colonel with fewer than 5,000.

Bruised but undaunted the reform forces decided to set up a "City Reform Association" after the election. In November they held a general meeting and, "earnestly inviting the cooperation of their fellow-citizens," wrote Scharf, they presented the voters with a program for better government. For months nothing happened of any consequence though Wallis continued to publish his trenchant editorials. However, as the elections of fall 1859 approached, the people's interest and concern grew. Early in September the association staged a mass meeting with some 10,000 persons filling Monument Square and the nearby streets. It announced that its prime aims were to put up a slate of decent municipal candidates and to police all elections. In October it scored its first success; its candidates for the city council carried six wards out of the city's twenty. It was no landslide but it was impressive.

Glowering at this opposition the Know-Nothings went all out to win the statewide election of the next month. It was for this election that they held their own rally at the Battle Monument

6. Scharf, *Chronicles of Baltimore,* p. 563.

and heard Henry Winter Davis orate surrounded by awls. On election day they stopped at nothing and they won. Concerning his own ward Wallis coldly reported: "About twenty minutes or a half an hour after the polls were opened in the tenth ward, they were taken forcible possession of by . . . rioters with a volley of bricks and a discharge of fire-arms; from that time until I left, no man was permitted access to the polls except at the pleasure of the 'Know-Nothing party.' " [7] Wallis also attested to the cooping which went on, observing that a political boss in his locality collected thirty or forty men in his house— "a wretched set of creatures, filthy, stupefied with drink"—and dragged them to the polls at least half a dozen times. [8]

Though the Baltimore Know-Nothings won the battle it turned out that they lost the war. Two weeks after the election the outraged Reform Association met and voted to present to the house of delegates the massive evidence of fraud it had assembled. It also voted to form a committee to draft better election laws. Wallis was named to the committee. It drafted the laws with dispatch and offered them to the house, which, thanks in part to Wallis's enthusiastic lobbying, readily enacted them. Moreover, the house found the evidence of fraud overwhelming and annulled its results by expelling nine Know-Nothing delegates from Baltimore chosen in the tainted election.

In August 1860 the reformers put forward a full slate and moved through the campaign with most of their fellow citizens behind them. Even the Know-Nothing clubs, daunted by citywide indignation, became less rowdy. The reform candidate for mayor, George William Brown, an energetic, aristocratic-looking lawyer with a cavalry mustache, and all the reform candidates for city council won by heavy majorities. As Wallis declared afterward in a speech at the Maryland Institute, "Red-handed murder no longer writes election returns among us." [9] Now many a Baltimorean thought he could look forward to a period of political peace.

7. Scharf, *Chronicles of Baltimore*, p. 571.
8. Quoted in Carleton Beals, *Brass-Knuckle Crusade: The Great Know-Nothing Conspiracy, 1820–1860* (New York: Hastings House, 1960), p. 191.
9. Wallis, "Speech at the Maryland Institute, February 1, 1861," *Writings*, 2: 132.

4

Black, White, and Gray

11. John Thompson: Mere Existence

*P*OLITICS bulked large in mid-nineteenth-century Maryland; the newspapers could hardly print enough about it. But daily life bulked larger. And its range was wide. We might look at a little of it at each extreme, as reflected in a slave narrative at one end and the domestic letters of a well-to-do white couple at the other.

Happy slaves have seldom left histories. Perhaps there were more such slaves than we think but the brute fact remains that they were human beings owned by other human beings. Most slaves submitted to existing as property; they had little choice. A few fled, among them John Thompson. *The Life of John Thompson, a Fugitive Slave* was printed in Worcester, Massachusetts, in 1856. It's an often harrowing account; that's why the abolitionists published it. But its general accuracy can be checked against other slave narratives. Its incidents and episodes turn out to be all too typical.[1]

"I was born in Maryland in 1812," Thompson begins, "and was slave to Mrs. Wagar." Apparently the Wagars were

---

1. John Thompson, *The Life of John Thompson, a Fugitive Slave, Containing His History of 25 Years in Bondage and His Providential Escape* (Worcester, Mass.: J. Thompson, 1856).

wealthy planters. Thompson's parents were field hands, his younger sister a maid in the Wagar house. His first understanding of what slavery meant came when his older sister was sold. His mother trudged to the slave trader's house with her other children, knelt in tears at the door, and begged to see her daughter before she was sent away. The trader let them in; there was the sister already in chains. When they embraced, their grief was so great that the trader himself was moved. At nightfall when they were finally to be separated, the trader told the daughter that she could walk back a way if she promised to return. To the mother he said, "Old woman, I will do the best I can for your daughter; I will sell her to a good master." [2] Her family never saw her again. Later they learned that she'd been taken to Alabama and hawked at public auction.

The working day at the Wagar plantation opened at dawn, shortly after the overseer's horn sounded over the cabins. All the slaves labored in the fields except the lucky handful helping around the Wagar house. Season after season they sowed, cultivated, and reaped. There were three main crops: corn, wheat, and the inevitable tobacco. The tobacco was often infested by tobacco worms, which got to be about two inches long, according to Thompson. These the slaves had to find and pick off. If they missed one, Mr. Wagar made them eat it. The food the Wagars allotted each slave per week was a peck of corn, two dozen herrings, and about four pounds of meat. This was a more nourishing ration, incidentally, than most.

A woman at Wagar's was allowed four weeks of rest following childbirth. After that she went back to the fields and her baby had to be cared for by her older children if she had any. If she didn't, she had to "take her child with her to the field, place it at the side where she could see it as she came to the end of the row, moving it along as she moved from row to row." [3]

Some owners were better than the Wagars, some worse. A good many slaves knew from experience because they were sold, and sold more than once. The slave trade in Maryland was

2. Thompson, *Life*, p. 15.
3. Thompson, *Life*, p. 17.

brisk. On Mrs. Wagar's death in 1822 the Thompson family was bought by a George Thomas, who "fed his slaves well but drove and whipped them most unmercifully." George Thomas could afford to feed them well; his plantation covered a thousand acres. His favorite way of whipping, John Thompson found, was to have the slave tied around a hogshead so that he lay helpless and then to use the lash. Thompson wrote that he saw one sturdy slave whipped till "his entrails could be seen moving within his body."

Even as a child Thompson showed that he had a lively mind. Before he left the Wagar plantation he learned the rudiments of reading and writing. A friendly white boy, a poor relation of the Wagars, taught him out of Webster's spelling book and the first and second English readers. "My little teacher improved every chance that offered of giving his instructions."

By the time he reached his teens Thompson was capable enough so that George Thomas could hire him out at a profit. Such hiring was frequent and Thompson himself obviously took it for granted. One year George Thomas hired him out to a neighbor, a man named Compton, known as "a kind master, feeding and clothing well, and seldom beating his slaves." Next Thompson was hired out to another kind master who lived about thirty-five miles away. Working for him was the most pleasant experience Thompson had as a slave. The other planters in the vicinity were as humane as this one. The land was fertile, the labor not tasking. Many of the jobs that poor whites ordinarily did the blacks were allowed to do here. And they often did them better than what Thompson contemptuously calls the "miserable, loafing white people." The planters even permitted some of their slaves to be schooled, so Thompson could continue his studying openly. Most significant for him and his fellows was that they were allowed the comforts of religion. In fact the planters had a church built for them and provided a white preacher. The church flourished. "Many white people went here to hear the colored ones sing and praise God."

Unfortunately his current master, who was single, moved to Prince Georges County, "a neighborhood as different from that which we had just left as Alabama is from Kentucky," where he married a rich, cruel wife. He arranged to take along the entire Thompson family. He even made Thompson's father the overseer and when the father died appointed one of the sons to succeed him. But his wife repeatedly beat Thompson's mother, who was her cook, "with shovel, tongs, or whatever other weapon lay within her reach." He writes that his emotion "upon hearing her shrieks and pleadings may better be imagined than described." [4]

We can see the economic range of Maryland planters in his experience alone. More than once he worked for a planter as wealthy as the Wagars with their hundreds of slaves. At the opposite extreme he was once hired out to someone called Hughes who owned only a single slave. Hughes supplemented the slave with a few hired hands, black and white, like Thompson but they were so few that everyone ate around the same kitchen table.

Because he was a black who could read and write he was suspected as time went on of using his pen to forge passes for other slaves who hoped to escape to the North. These passes were travel permits made out and signed by whites which the slaves had to carry any time they left their home plantations. One Monday, after a weekend when he himself had been allowed off the plantation, he three times heard a voice warning him not to return. So he walked over to an uncle's cabin. His uncle told him that two constables were waiting at the plantation to arrest him. As Thompson explained gratefully, "I knew it was the hand of God, working in my behalf; it was his voice warning me to escape from the danger towards which I was hastening." [5] He fell on his knees to give thanks and then began his tortuous way to freedom.

On the road from southern Maryland to the North he repeatedly came close to capture, including one time outside of Rockville. Often he traveled through the hostile countryside at night, usually with a black guide. At times Thompson lost the way, most notably when instead of walking straight north he wandered west as far as Frederick and then back east to Baltimore.

4. Thompson, *Life,* p. 49.
5. Thompson, *Life,* p. 80.

Because of this interminable walking his feet and ankles swelled so much that he had to rest periodically, far longer than he wished. However, one night shortly before dawn he reached the state line. It was where the Baltimore turnpike entered Pennsylvania, near a town now called New Freedom. He tramped into the daylight, "rejoicing and praising God for this deliverance."

12. The Prestons: Everyday Life

"Burn my letters . . . they are intended for you alone," Madge Preston cautioned her "dear and precious husband." But he didn't, so we still see not only words of love but also a host of details about daily life in upper middle-class Maryland. If not the rock-bottom routines like the times the Prestons went to bed or got up, then the next thing to it: information about vacation trips, business affairs, marital misunderstandings, child raising, meetings with notables, household management, and head colds. Informative if not terribly exciting.

The Prestons, William and Margaret, were white and prosperous. They were married in August 1846. She was both younger and more affectionate than he; William was something of a stick. There's an early painting of him; it shows us a rather handsome man with a petulant mouth and a haughty expression.[1] Yet he had one inclination the reverse of stodgy: an attorney by profession, he relished defending men accused of murder. Before he retired in the 1870s, he'd acted as counsel in more than a hundred homicide cases. He also did a good deal of civil litigation. His office was in Baltimore on Fayette Street. His permanent avocation was politics, his party Democratic. His wife spent most of her time at their attractive farm called Pleasant Plains, on the Hillen Road between Towson and Baltimore City. Her roles were typical: wife, mother, housekeeper, hostess; they kept her busy. However, she got away every now and then, traveling most often to Philadelphia, where her family lived. Anyhow she liked her life and said so.

---

1. Portrait of William P. Preston, 1835; artist unknown; Maryland Historical Society, Baltimore.

William's work took him away regularly from Pleasant Plains. He drove back and forth to Baltimore enough to qualify as a commuter. As he built up his practice he also made trips to Philadelphia, Washington, and even New York. The result was that Madge wrote him voluminously and frequently. She loved to put pen to paper, she confessed. So for that matter did he, though he couldn't match her output. Much of their domestic correspondence, far from having been burned, now rests in the McKeldin Library at the University of Maryland.

We might start our sampling of it early in their marriage. "My dear and precious husband," Madge begins a letter she pens from Westminster, Maryland, on July 18, 1847, while she herself is traveling. The letter is warmed throughout by her love for Preston, as she describes to him the vicissitudes of life on the road. She's arrived late in Westminster because their coach-man, Anderson, hadn't fed the horses breakfast. By the time they'd drawn the carriage ten miles along the Baltimore turn-pike, the road which led through Reisterstown to Westminster and beyond, the horses were obviously tired. So Madge had ordered a stop although her husband's instructions had been to wait till Reisterstown. "If I go contrary to your directions, it is because I feel the circumstances of the case require me to do so," she explains tactfully. She adds that a contrite Anderson has now carefully washed off and fed the horses and rubbed them down.

Here and there she sketches the summer scenery for Preston. In one place the hillocks of hay in the green meadows look like Indian villages to her. Her imagination peoples them with braves and dark-eyed maidens. She ends the letter fervently, "May God bless and protect my kind, good husband till he meets again his little Lassie."

She's still away from home and now visiting relatives when she writes a letter of August 1. Preston is at work in Baltimore and she urges him to escape the city and join her. The neighbors and relatives, especially her two small nieces, would delight to see him. If he comes, incidentally, could he bring along a simple ring for each niece? Rings remind her of the fact that their wedding anniversary, August 12, is approaching. "I have always intended, if possible,'' she writes, ''to pass that day throughout our lives together.''

We might look at a letter from Preston next, perhaps the one for November 14. He and Madge have been apart, and she's written that she's not only missed him but his letters while she's been away. She's begun to wonder whether she means anything to him. He tells her ''very candidly'' that, contrary to her notion that he thinks her ''absence an advantage'' and that she isn't necessary to him, he's found Pleasant Plains gloomy indeed without her. He laments the fact that its silence has been unbroken by the music of her voice. He can't understand her feeling. ''Ah me,'' he philosophizes, women ''are strange creatures— governed by strange impulses—say strange things.'' Regardless, he yearns to have her home with him.

The domestic high point for the Prestons during the next few years is the birth of May, who proves to be their only child. Naturally there's much about her in the correspondence. Otherwise the Prestons' homelife progresses uneventfully. Its pleasures are peaceful ones; the social life is informal. Every now and then there's a foray into the city to take advantage of its cultural attractions. For instance on September 18, 1852, Preston dashes off a note to Madge, ''Tonight there will be a fine opera and if you feel a disposition to see it you have a fine day to come.''

But business has more claims than pleasure at this point in American life; and Preston sends Madge a letter, characteristic of many, saying that he won't be home because there's a 4:00 P.M. session of court in Baltimore. The letter is dated November 17, 1852, and comes from his room at Barnum's—to Charles Dickens in *American Notes* the ''most comfortable of all the hotels of which I had any experience in the United States.'' He's busy defending one Michael Rock, charged with murder, and that's why he's had scarcely a moment to spare.

By the time the Prestons have been married for half a dozen years, Madge's ''dear and precious husband'' has become ''dear Mr. Preston'' in the salutations. But her love seems undiminished. She writes from Pleasant Plains on April 7, 1853, describing how she's hoped all day that he'll be home that evening. Their carriage drove up but without him in it. There was a letter from him, though, and she "seized it with the avidity they always inspire." She had finished scanning only the first page "when up drove Judge Legrand and his aunt. Think, dear husband, what I suffered while they were here." Perhaps her self-denial will count for something since it's now the Lenten season. But Lent or not, she offers the judge and his aunt "a good cup of coffee accompanied with sundry viands such as cold boiled chicken, strawberry preserves, . . . nice fresh bread, and sweet, good butter." She finishes reading the letter after they leave. It includes Preston's account of a splendid dinner party he attended, with many intellectuals among the guests; and Madge exclaims, "It is my pride that even amidst these giants of the mind, my husband thrives conspicuous and his genius and his eloquence make their mark *even there.*"

Preston composes a long letter on July 14, 1853. Madge has written disconsolately that he might at least have penned a line to her while she was gone from home and he was in Baltimore. Indignantly he answers that he's already penned not one letter but three. Don't blame him if they haven't arrived; blame the mails. Anyway he now writes boldly across the top of the first sheet "Fourth Letter." He has plenty of news to relate. Three days earlier the new president, Franklin Pierce, visited Baltimore. Preston as a fellow Democrat was delighted by the enthusiasm with which Baltimore greeted him. He reports proudly that the next morning he breakfasted with the president and the cabinet members traveling with him. Secretary of War Jefferson Davis impressed him most. He had "that straightforward, whole-souled sincerity which peculiarly belongs to the Southern character and in which there is none of the inflexible hardness and prying calculation of Plymouth Rock."

Preston goes on to tell of the comings and goings at Pleasant Plains, to complain about May's nursemaid for being awkward and careless, to say that Polly has been doing the washing and ironing, and to note that the farmhands have been making hay. He mentions that their friend Mrs. Morris has just given birth to a boy but that Mr. Morris has said sadly that it probably wouldn't live. Preston drops a number of pronouncements into the middle part of the letter, such as "Courage is the immediate offspring of the highest virtues" and "An aged person like an aged tree is but little able to bear up against the storms or shocks of fate." Toward the end of the letter he turns to politics, in this case his campaign for the Democratic nomination for Congress in the Third District, where he's opposing a veteran politician, Joshua Vansant. Then, reverting to domestic matters, he urges Madge to see that good care is taken of the horse Jupiter and that people don't drive him too much. He concludes by sending his love and enclosing some of the new stamped envelopes, "a good contrivance to replace loose stamps."

On May 1, 1854, there's a quick note telling her to use the green carriage and Jupiter. There's another note, of February 7, 1855, in which he mutters about having to work too hard and having gotten a headache the day before. Then there's a four-page letter to Madge dated April 7, 1855, and sent from Jones' Hotel in Philadelphia. It intersperses its news with some of his usual dictums, for example, "The juice, however expressed, from those grapes which we gather on the wayside of existence not infrequently improves with age." The news includes the fact that he's been ill and that the illness has depressed him; that he's been theater-going nevertheless, and has seen *Hamlet* played beautifully; and that he must shortly travel on business either to the Pennsylvania coal fields or to New York.

Madge likewise enjoyed the theater. In a letter of March 29, 1856, she describes going to the Museum Theater in Baltimore to attend the farewell benefit for one of its veteran stars, Joe Cowell. Then she speaks of a Philadelphia couple named Swain, who've been hospitable to Preston. She wants to return their hospitality and is hurt and mortified that she hasn't been able to. As soon as warm weather comes the Swains must visit Pleasant Plains to enjoy a respite "from the busy turmoil of city life." She closes with love and a wifely caution that Preston should "*go to bed early.*"

His reply of April 3 makes the reason for the caution plain. He's been plagued by one of his worst head colds in years. He appreciates her "physic and good advice," he says, adding that her letters are always "gratifying and welcome." We know that they were and continued to be. In his diary a dozen years later he grumbles to himself, "Disappointed that I have received no letter from Mrs. Preston." [2] The distance between their affectionate and comfortable homelife and John Thompson's existence was astronomical.

13. More Free than Less

A significant part of Maryland's daily life prior to the Civil War has to do with slaves and masters. Too often we think of blacks in bondage, of whites wielding whips. There's another group of blacks we almost never think of, the free ones. Their number was astonishing. Perhaps the most unexpected statistic in Maryland history comes from the federal census of 1860; it counted 87,189 slaves and 83,942 free blacks. We had more than any other state in the Union.

Ordinarily they were free either because a master had manumitted them or because they'd been born of freed parents. A minute percentage were able to buy their own freedom. Freeing began almost as soon as slavery itself. In Maryland it was sometimes a trickle, at other times a stream; the extent sometimes depended on the statutes, at other times on the prevailing currents of opinion. We can guess that frequently a master freed a slave either out of gratitude or guilt. The gratitude might be for faithful service, the guilt because of the feeling that it was wrong for one human being to be a chattel to another. Or the guilt might come from the fact that the master had sired the slave. Sometimes the reason was a miserly one: the master might free an ailing slave to get rid of him. Or an elderly slave for the same reason. That happened often enough so that the state passed a law forbidding the freeing of slaves past forty-five.

Not that most masters ever considered freeing any slave. Far from it. In *The Free Negro in Maryland, 1634–1860*, James Wright surveys the statues designed to cut back freeing or root it

2. Diary of William P. Preston, entry of June 27, 1868; Preston Papers, Maryland Historical Society. Used with permission.

out entirely. The first important one, passed in 1752 and on the books till 1790, prohibited freeing slaves not only through a master's oral declaration, which had already from time to time been barred, but through his written will. This had become one of the most frequent forms, with the master specifying that his slave or slaves should be released on his death. The last, and severest, statute was passed in 1860 by the assembly but emphatically rejected by the voters. It would have ended all freeing.[1]

The leading advocate of that statute was a hot-blooded slaveowner from the Eastern Shore, Col. Curtis Jacobs. However, he went far beyond mere prohibition. An ardent foe of the free black, he served as chairman of the house of delegates' committee on the colored population. In a speech of February 17, 1860, to the house, which liked it so well that it ordered it published as a pamphlet, he denounced every aspect of what he termed "free-Negroism." [2] The speech opened with a eulogy of our country as a whole, switched to a denunciation of the North, and then expatiated on what had to be done with free blacks. About that he was nothing if not thorough.

"Free-Negroism throughout this state," he said resoundingly, "must be abolished. A universal pass system must be adopted. Emancipation by last will and testament, or by any other means, must be prohibited. Negro worship, except in the assembly of the white congregation, and at the stated place and hours for the same, must not be allowed. Free Negroes going out of the state must not be allowed to return on pain of being sold into slavery for life. No free Negro to enter the state, under a like penalty. Negroes must not be allowed to attend political meetings, elections, fairs, or other public gatherings. A general police system throughout the state, to enforce and execute those and such other needful laws on the subject, must be provided for. A close system of espionage upon all stragglers and strangers of no known pursuit must be observed." [3]

1. James Wright, *The Free Negro in Maryland, 1634–1860* (New York: Columbia University, 1921), pp. 39, 325.
2. Curtis Jacobs, "Speech of Col. Curtis M. Jacobs on the Free Colored Population of Maryland" (Annapolis: Elihu S. Riley, 1860).
3. Jacobs, "Speech," p. 7.

Affirming that free blacks weren't citizens but aliens, Colonel Jacobs triumphantly listed their current disabilities in Maryland. They ranged from resale into slavery for a minor crime to such harassments as not being able to keep a dog without an official license from the justice of the peace. In concluding his speech to his fellow delegates he affirmed, "Having in view the fear of God, the wishes of a confiding constituency, and the lasting welfare of this state, there remains but little else for me to do but cast my vote in favor of the passage of the bill." [4]

The Jacobs Bill, as it became known throughout Maryland, passed in the house 41 to 3 and in the senate without a single dissent. But it had to be ratified by the counties, and when the fall elections came they threw it back in the assembly's face. They rejected it by more than three to one. Even in Worcester County, the home of the colonel's "confiding constituency," the vote was 1,217 against and 842 for. If we relied on the fiery oratory of politicians like Jacobs we couldn't comprehend why Maryland sheltered more free blacks than any other state. But when we look at the balloting we see how widespread toleration was; for the bill carried only in Somerset County and lost in every other one, most crushingly in Baltimore County, where the vote was 5,354 against and 681 for.

Still, the elected rulers of Maryland hedged in the free blacks with regulations up until the Civil War. These operated ordinarily through the orphans' courts. The Maryland Historical Society has a small file of "Free Negro Papers" which illustrate some of the regulations. On movement, for one. The rulers of Maryland made it clear that they didn't want free blacks moving in. In fact they didn't want any blacks, slave or free, moving anywhere except at the convenience of the whites. The result was the increasingly elaborate system of passes. For free blacks the passes had to come from an official. Jacob Henderson's survives in the Free Negro file. It was issued by the orphans' court of Cecil County on February 10, 1847, and permitted him to visit friends in Pennsylvania for a week or two. Three whites signed for him. Isabella Harris's pass likewise survives. She too

4. Jacobs, "Speech," p. 31.

wished to travel outside of Maryland and then return. In October 1849 the orphans' court granted permission; four whites vouched for her. To prevent any trading in passes, the pass described her: "free Negro . . . aged about forty years, of dark complexion, five feet four inches high, without any noticeable marks or scars."

"The function of the Negro in Maryland was to do manual labor," Wright observed.[5] This was as true for free blacks as for slaves. Moreover, many a free black continued to do the same work, almost like an indentured servant, that he'd done before. In many cases that was all he could do. If he could support his family it was by a meager margin, and if he died his widow could rarely support their children.

The result was that the state stepped in. It assumed that the widow could somehow take care of herself but that the children were another matter. More and more black orphans and children of free blacks without support were bound out as apprentices by court order. For instance little William Henry. His paper is one of those in the Cecil County file. With his mother's consent the justices of the peace bound him out in 1825, when he was seven, to Elijah Reynolds. It was stipulated that William would work hard and behave himself. In return Reynolds would teach him the "art of farming." He would support William fully while training him, would "cause him to be taught to read, write, and cast up accounts," and when he ended his apprenticeship at twenty-one would give him a suit of clothes and $25.

William was typical of the boys; the "Negro . . . Mary, being a free colored orphan," was typical of the girls. Her indenture is dated April 9, 1833. When she was eight the Cecil County Orphans' Court bound her out to another Reynolds, James this time. She too was supposed to work hard. In return James Reynolds would train her as a servant, would see to it that she learned to read the New Testament and was raised a Christian, and would support her fully. When at eighteen she ended her apprenticeship, he would supply her with "one new suit of apparel," plus shoes and stockings.

5. Wright, *The Free Negro*, p. 130.

There's another revealing document in the file, a summons, dated June 12, 1844. Three free blacks from Cecil County, Mat Anderson, Sam Anderson, and Perry McCurd, along with their children, are ordered to appear in court on the charge of being "without visible means of subsistence." There's also a memo sheet for the constable so that he can bring them in if need be. If the charge against them was correct they could be convicted of vagrancy. The court could order them to leave the state—by a statute of 1825 they had fifteen days to do that—or to go to jail or to work for a white employer for up to a year. Though it's true that convictions weren't numerous the threat was always there.

It was Wright's opinion that "aside from the coercion of the vagrancy laws the free Negro enjoyed a wide liberty in getting a living." [6] For a time this was true, both for unskilled and more or less skilled labor. As the slave population shrank, on the Eastern Shore and in southern Maryland generally, the use of free blacks rose. The women did washing, cooking, cleaning, and sometimes field work. Most men were field hands; some did other hard and unskilled labor. A smaller number got semi-skilled jobs, as carters, handlers, or warehousemen, for example. A still smaller number, mainly in Baltimore, got skilled jobs. Barbering, blacksmithing, and calking were the most popular crafts but Wright lists more than two dozen which some free blacks followed. [7]

However, the jobs for free blacks shrank in the 1840s and 1850s, especially in Baltimore, The attractions of urban life, plus the economic advantages, were growing clearer all the time and to all sorts of people. We can recall that Baltimore was becoming Mecca. Both whites and blacks were being drawn from rural to urban Maryland. Also, the tide of immigration from Europe was setting in, and the typical European immigrant stayed in the city rather than venturing into the countryside. Because he was poor and ill-spoken he had to start with the most menial jobs but then he was apt to work himself upward.

6. Wright, *The Free Negro*, p. 97.
7. Wright, *The Free Negro*, p. 155.

Such free blacks as Mat and Sam Anderson might leave Cecil County for Baltimore but, once there, they had to fight harder and harder competition. And they were heavily handicapped by their color and slave culture. By the 1850s the blacks who had loaded ships or shoveled coal or done a score of the sweatiest jobs in the city were being crowded out by the whites. Even in the crafts which the blacks had made their own, such as ship calking or oyster shucking, the whites gradually took over. They tried rioting, when necessary, to capture the blacks' jobs and they succeeded.[8] Economically speaking the blacks became all too often, to use the title of recent book, "slaves without masters." On the other hand, no one owned them; no one had the power of life or death over them; they were far better off than before.

8. Wright, *The Free Negro,* p. 172.

5

Wallis and the Wars: Military and Political

14. Bloody Streets

*A*FTER the reformers finally demolished the Know-Nothings in the election of fall 1860, many a Baltimorean doubtless thought that he could look forward, as we said earlier, to a long period of political peace. He couldn't have been more wrong. `

At the same time that a local calm was setting in, a nationwide storm was gathering. Its portents were all too plain if Baltimoreans wanted to see them, for without leaving town they could watch three of the four national political conventions being wracked with dissension over states' rights and slavery. In May 1860 the remnants of the Know-Nothings and Whigs—now calling themselves the Constitutional Union party—met at the old Presbyterian church on the corner of North and Fayette streets, tried to pull things together, and nominated John Bell of Tennessee for president. In mid-June the regular Democrats, already fragmented, met at the Front Street Theater, only to fragment again. Finally they nominated Stephen Douglas of Illinois. After the adjournment of the regular Democrats, the secessionist Democrats met at the Maryland Institute and nominated John Breckinridge of Kentucky. Meanwhile, in Chicago the bustling young Republicans nominated Abraham Lincoln of Illinois, who went on to win in November by 180 electoral votes to Breckinridge's 72, Bell's 39, and Douglas's 12. In Maryland, Breckinridge and Bell, both calling for concessions to the South to save the Union, came out far ahead. Breckinridge won the popular vote by 42,842 to Bell's 41,760. Lincoln got a trifling 2,294.

Step by step the nation neared war. In December outgoing President Buchanan said helplessly in his message to Congress that the Southern states had no right to secede but that the Federal government had no power to prevent them. Two weeks later South Carolina seceded; during January 1861 the five Gulf states and Georgia followed.

The position of the Border states, Maryland perhaps most of all, was agonizing. Maryland's meager vote for Lincoln was deceptive. When the hour of decision came, about whether to join the North or the South, the state was divided to its depths. Wallis was one of many in feeling profoundly disturbed. The only proper way out, he decided, was to have the Constitution amended to protect slavery from any future interference. This was what a special committee of the House of Representatives proposed while the Southern states were seceding; this was what he publicly endorsed.

At a mass meeting on February 1 at the Maryland Institute he made a speech, long, eloquent, and impassioned, in favor of a statewide convention to support the House proposal. He and many of his hearers had already asked the Know-Nothing governor, Thomas Hicks, to call such a convention. They felt that it would reveal an overwhelming sentiment in the state for the amendment. Hicks had wavered about Maryland's role, first inclining toward the South and then toward the North. Originally he argued that the Border states, among them Maryland, had the strength to hold the Union together if they wished, because they were the pivotal states. If the North's politicians refused to amend the Constitution Maryland should join the seceders, he said. But later he shifted his position; and Wallis could now charge that Hicks hoped to keep Maryland "inert and silent" till Lincoln's inauguration and after that to lure the state, through its devotion to the Union, into espousing the Republican party. When Wallis painted this repellent prospect his hearers cried "Never, never." [1]

Speaking as a lawyer Wallis went on to assure his audience that the Constitution didn't require any state to stay in the Union. Speaking as a Marylander with Southern ties, he scorned the idea of forcing Southerners to stay, the idea that he and his audience should "go among them with fire and sword, and . . . ravage and despoil their heritage in order that they may love us and cleave to us hereafter." [2]

As the weeks went along it grew clear that though Wallis's views were endorsed by many, many others opposed them. There were as frequent mass meetings for the governor as against him. The state's political leadership showed itself to be similarly divided. Wallis, for instance, stood on one side while his old friend and guide Reverdy Johnson stood on the other. Before the end of February the South had organized its Confederate Congress and picked a provisional president, Jefferson Davis. But Maryland hung back.

That same month Lincoln was scheduled to pass through the state and stop in Baltimore on his way from Springfield, Illinois, to Washington for the inauguration. Baltimore, though, was the only city on his route to refuse him a welcoming delegation. More forbidding was the fact that Pinkerton detectives told him when he reached Philadelphia of a rumored plot to assassinate him in Baltimore. One or two members of his new official family told him likewise that they believed in the possibility of a plot. No evidence of it has ever surfaced. However, on the evening of February 22 he and his bodyguard boarded the last sleeping car of the night train to Baltimore, on which a female Pinkerton detective had reserved berths for her "invalid brother" and his companion. Around three in the morning the car was drawn through the Baltimore streets between depots. Supposedly at one point Lincoln heard a drunkard singing "Dixie." At six he stepped off the train in Washington.

1. Wallis, "Speech at the Maryland Institute," *Writings,* 2: 130.
2. Wallis, "Speech at the Maryland Institute," *Writings,* 2: 137.

On Baltimore streets on April 19 the first bloodshed of the
Civil War took place. Four soldiers and twelve Baltimoreans
were killed outright; a number of wounded died afterward. Two
days before, Mayor George William Brown, seeing signs of
trouble that he'd known all too well from the Know-Nothing
riots, had issued a proclamation calling for calm. On the eighteenth the first Northern troops, ordered south to quell what Lincoln was terming the "insurrection," passed through the city. A
force of 600 Pennsylvanians, they had to march from the depot
at the corner of Cathedral and Howard streets to the Mount
Clare depot. Although hooting, yelling crowds lined the route
there was no violence. Early the next day rumors spread that
another and larger Northern force was coming. The chief of
police, or marshal, was Col. George Kane, a burly soldier and
businessman who'd proved his mettle during the reform campaigns. He did his utmost that day to keep order. At eleven in
the morning a train of thirty-five cars pulled in with 2,000 troops
aboard. They too had to change trains to go south but this time
the plan was to do it by horsecar. The route from the Philadelphia depot to the Camden station was about a mile long and bor-
dered with more jeering crowds. After letting several cars
through, but pelting the last one with stones, the crowd at the
Gay Street crossing tore up some of the car tracks and laid
anchors across others.

The Federal commanders ordered the remaining troops to
move by foot through the streets. Here is Scharf's vigorous account of what followed: "They were formed into [a] column
four abreast, with an escort of police at front and rear. . . .
They had not proceeded far when a volley of stones was thrown
into their ranks. . . . The troops now quickened their pace to a
run, holding down their heads to avoid the flying stones and
bricks. . . . At East Falls Avenue they were joined by Mayor
Brown, who, thinking his presence might restrain the mob, at
great risk to his life, placed himself at the head of the column
and marched with them. . . . When the head of the column
reached the crossing of Commerce Street their march was
checked by a dense crowd, completely blocking the way, who
gave vent to their wrath in a furious yell and showered a volley

of paving-stones upon the troops. . . . At this moment the commanding officer gave the order to fire, and at the first discharge a citizen fell. An irregular fusillade was now kept up on the crowd, killing and wounding a number of persons. . . . One citizen was forced by the rush of the crowd close to the troops. A soldier, raising his musket, took deliberate aim at him, but the piece missed fire, on which the citizen sprang upon him, wrenched the musket from his hands, and plunged the bayonet through his body. . . . The troops again pressed forward at a run, still firing occasionally, the crowd closing in behind them. Near Light Street Marshal Kane threw a picked body of police, with drawn revolvers, across the street and checked the further advance of the mob. Their rear thus guarded, the troops reached Camden Station in safety.'' [3]

In what became our state song young James Ryder Randall cried:

> Avenge the patriotic gore
> That flecked the streets of Baltimore,
> And be the battle queen of yore,
> Maryland! My Maryland!

And in his final stanza he exulted about Maryland, ''Huzza! she spurns the Northern scum.'' Many Marylanders exulted with him; again, many Marylanders didn't.

Only the extremists on either side welcomed bloodshed. Attempts at compromise continued to be made. After the riot Mayor Brown sent at least two committees to Lincoln at the White House, heading one himself which included Wallis, to seek an accommodation which would keep Federal troops from passing through Baltimore. In Annapolis Governor Hicks grudgingly agreed to call an emergency session of the assembly even if not a statewide citizens' convention about joining the Confederacy. Also he named April 24 as the day for Baltimoreans to choose delegates to replace the Know-Nothings expelled for being elected by fraud. A single slate of civic leaders, Wallis among them, was elected unopposed. Because Federal troops

---

3. Scharf, *History of Baltimore*, pp. 789–790.

had recently occupied Annapolis the assembly moved to Frederick in protest, where it met at the county courthouse for a day and then moved to better quarters in the new German Reformed hall. Wallis was chosen chairman of the key house of delegates' committee on federal relations. From the outset the sentiment was largely antisecessionist, for assorted reasons ranging from fear of Federal force to love for the Union. At the end of April the delegates approved 53 to 12 a report he drafted, in answer to a petition from Prince Georges citizens, which declared that the house had no power to pass an ordinance of secession. Two weeks later the delegates approved another report, also drafted by Wallis, which declared against a statewide convention on the secession question.

However, the language of that report shows plainly that the concessions to the North were being made with growing bitterness. The report stigmatized Lincoln's calling out of the troops as "a deliberate summons to the people of the two sections into which his party and its principles had so hopelessly divided the land, to shed each other's blood in wantonness and hate." [4] It termed the resulting conflict an unholy war against people pleading only to be left alone. And it laid the blame even for the riot of April 19 at Lincoln's door because he had trampled on the Constitution. It concluded that because much of Maryland was then occupied by Federal troops, a statewide convention would be a sham.

As the tide of war rose in Maryland, leaders like Wallis became highly vulnerable. His stature grew as a fearless public figure; he remained outspoken for what he believed to be right and he used his caustic rhetoric against what he believed to be wrong. Unfortunately what he thought wrong was just about everything that Lincoln and his lieutenants were doing to hold Maryland, including: the occupation of Annapolis, just mentioned, by hard-nosed Gen. Benjamin Butler, who made his headquarters on the grounds of the Naval Academy; the suspension of the writ of habeas corpus in some parts of the state, so

4. Wallis, "Report of the Committee on Federal Relations in Regard to Calling a Sovereign Convention," *Writings,* 2: 151.

that the Federal army could arrest and imprison any persons it wished; and the occupation of Baltimore, on the evening of May 14, by Butler, who then established another headquarters on Federal Hill.

Nor was this all. In June Gen. Nathaniel Banks took command in Baltimore and shortly afterward was ordered to arrest the police commissioners, along with Marshal Kane, because they were suspected of being Southern sympathizers. To begin with he arrested only Kane. A detachment of Federal troops surrounded Kane's house, hustled him out, shoved him into a waiting hack, and spirited him to Fort McHenry, which fervent Federalists were already labeling "a depot for traitors."

On July 1 it was the commissioners' turn. Between two and three in the morning they were arrested at their homes and then likewise jailed in Fort McHenry. They asked Wallis to appeal to Congress on their behalf. He did so in a hard-hitting brief, also arguing that Kane had been unjustly imprisoned. Congress replied austerely that "military necessity" sanctioned the arrests. The sole remaining appeal lay to public opinion and the assembly made that, in another brief drafted by Wallis and dated August 5. He invoked the Declaration of Independence, the Constitution, and the Bill of Rights in attempting to show that the commissioners had done nothing lawless. The assembly endorsed his indignant statement, voting to send it to all members of Congress, all governors, and, through them, their state legislatures. Its general effect couldn't be measured. But it had one specific effect. It helped to assure the arrest of Wallis himself.

He was seized on the night of September 12 at his house on Saint Paul Street and watched in helpless outrage while the troopers ransacked his rooms and broke into locked drawers in the hope of finding incriminating papers, like correspondence with Confederate leaders. His arrest wasn't the only one that night. Federal soldiers seized the other members of the Baltimore City delegation to the legislature, the mayor of Baltimore, two delegates from Baltimore County, a state senator, a congressman, and two editors, one of whom was Francis Key Howard of the *Exchange*, the paper Wallis had been writing for. (On the 14th his friend William Glenn of the *Exchange* was likewise arrested.) The prisoners were first taken to Fort McHenry, the next afternoon to Fortress Monroe near Hampton Roads, two weeks later to Fort Lafayette in the harbor of New York City, and finally in November to Fort Warren in Boston Harbor. There he and a dozen other Marylanders were jailed for more than a year as "prisoners of state."

During that time he was assured that he would be freed if he signed a loyalty oath put before him which ended, "I will not do anything hostile to the United States during the insurrection." He answered in effect that he hadn't done anything hostile to begin with. In November 1862 he and his fellow prisoners were freed anyhow, without explanation or apology; they had become an embarrassment to the Lincoln administration.

A sickly man in his mid-forties, Wallis endured the privations of prison with fortitude. In fact he did more than that. The author of the introduction to his *Writings* observed, "By the charm of his conversation, bright and entertaining as if prison walls had no existence, he helped to beguile the tedium of a confinement which weighed heavily upon his companions as well as upon himself. By numberless acts of kindness and of charity, he contributed to alleviate the lot of others less fortunate and well-provided for than himself." [5] When the government let him and other "prisoners of state" have supplementary rations he made the arrangements. We can still find some of the bills in his papers, bills from the Boston grocers who sold him dozens of eggs, barrels of bass, and such other edibles as corn meal, lard, and mustard.

The government also allowed these prisoners such comforts as newspapers and books. Going back to the habit of his youth, Wallis snipped hundreds of items from the papers he had access to and ultimately filled four large clipping books while in jail. He had access to a wide variety of papers, plus plenty of time to read and clip. The Boston papers included the *Courier* and the *Transcript*, the New York ones the *Herald*, the *Tribune*, and the *Times*, and the Baltimore ones the Unionist *American* and the already eminent, Southern-leaning *Sun*. From the time

---

5. Anonymous introduction to *Writings*, 1: xviii.

of the first Battle of Bull Run the war went against the North, and he was able to clip a good share of reports of Southern victories despite the fact that most of the papers lent themselves to Northern propaganda. And he clipped all the Maryland and Baltimore stories he could discover. He savored the Southern victories but was saddened by the warfare in his home state.

15. Battleground

The Civil War scarred Maryland as no other war ever has. The state was occupied by the North and invaded by the South. And its internal dissensions were wrenching ones, even for those Marylanders not directly affected. At the end of 1862 William Preston wrote somberly that he hadn't "passed a quiet and happy hour" since the opening of the war.[1]

It's true that on the surface daily life went unimpeded for the most part and that recognized Union sympathizers could move about as they wished. Some of them moved quite profitably in fact, including the eminent merchant Enoch Pratt; for Baltimore enjoyed something of a boom in business from 1862 to 1865, thanks to Union spending. Millions of Federal dollars were paid out for military supplies, foodstuffs (especially flour), and transportation. The production of iron and copper items rose; shipbuilding increased.

Notwithstanding, the hard truth was that Maryland swiftly became an occupied territory, ruled by a succession of Union generals. Those generals loomed large in the popular mind. Some were sterner than others but they were perhaps epitomized by Ben Butler, whose drooping eyelid gave him a thoroughly sinister look. They governed directly by military force and indirectly by helping to install Union sympathizers in key political posts. Particularly in Baltimore they manipulated the election machinery with considerable effect and permitted political gangs to revive the Know-Nothing tradition of violence at the polls. They also systematically furloughed soldiers from the Union forces so that they could come home to cast their ballots.

1. Letter, William P. Preston to May Preston, December 22, 1862; Preston Papers, Maryland Historical Society. Used with permission.

Whatever degree of control the generals kept, they remained uneasy about the state's temper. Through both military orders and municipal ordinances they tried to stop any expressions, insignificant as well as significant, of feeling for the South. For instance in June 1862, as Scharf noted, "a young man and woman were arrested for waving a window curtain to some Confederate prisoners." [2] The publishers of popular music were ordered to end the sale of "secession music" because it was, to the provost marshal of that time, "evil, incendiary, and not for the public good." In another order shortly afterward he banned the sale of pictures of Southern generals and political leaders. To emphasize the positive he ordered three Baltimore congregations to display the Stars and Stripes during worship.

Such things were tokens at the most; we see an instance of more important actions when the city council, after being purged by the current commanding general, passed an ordinance making all school officials, including classroom teachers, take an oath of allegiance to the Union. If they refused they were to be dismissed. [3]

Yet these actions, military or civilian, were understandable. In the eyes of the Lincoln administration Maryland was a vital state: unless vigilance were unrelenting the state might defect to the South. Nobody knew then, and nobody knows now, whether the main sympathies lay with the North or the South. In some parts of the state it looked clear enough. The cities of Frederick and Hagerstown, for example, were patently loyal to the North; the counties of the Eastern Shore, going their own way as usual, were clearly devoted to the South. But about the state as a whole who could be sure?

More than once the administration tried to gauge its support in Maryland. But we might guess that the problem was complicated because both numbers and feelings were involved. That is, if the administration could have made a head count it might have showed that a majority of whites favored the North after the war got well under way. But their loyalty, by and large, appeared temperate and fires of abolitionist intensity burned in

2. Scharf, *History of Baltimore,* p. 139.
3. Scharf, *History of Baltimore,* p. 140.

only a few. The attachment to the South appeared often to be ardent, however. In fact even that early a Southern mystique was developing, traces of which we see today. And that could help to explain the Union generals' jumpiness.

Ex-Confederate that he was, Scharf exemplified the mystique in his histories, for instance when suggesting that, though thousands of Marylanders fought well on both sides, those on the Southern side had higher motives and were better men. He claimed that these men weren't formed into divisions or even brigades by the Confederates because "they were required to officer companies, regiments, and brigades of troops from other states; for, as a general thing, the young men from Maryland were of a superior order intellectually, . . . were actuated by patriotism alone, and not driven into the service by the conscript officer or influenced by mercenary motives." [4] Actually there were Confederate regiments made up of Marylanders, beginning with the First Maryland Infantry, C. S. A., led by the dashing, goateed Bradley Johnson of Frederick; but Scharf was right about the wide dispersal of Marylanders in the Confederate armies.

As the war spread and then intensified, Maryland got its fill of fighting. The war divided not only regions, races, and classes but even families. It was fact, not fiction, that sometimes father fought against son, brother against brother. In Winchester, just before the Battle of Gettysburg, Maj. William Goldsborough of the Second Maryland Infantry, C. S. A., captured his own brother, a surgeon in the Fifth Maryland Federals.

The outright military actions came often. There was a welter of skirmishing and battling as the armies marched or rode back and forth across the state. Central Maryland was especially vulnerable because the Shenandoah Valley offered an inviting avenue into Virginia for the Northern forces and into Maryland for the Southern ones: it was a busy two-way street. The most memorable collision on Maryland soil, and a stunning one, was the Battle of Antietam, a dozen miles from where the Shenandoah River joined the Potomac.

4. Scharf, *Chronicles of Baltimore,* p. 649.

There were three major Confederate incursions into Maryland, one each year. The first took place early in September 1862. Having beaten the Federal forces at the second Battle of Bull Run, sending them trekking back toward Washington, Gen. Robert E. Lee decided to invade the North. In the glow of optimism coming from his victory he planned to get as far as Harrisburg. There he intended to destroy the important railroad bridge across the Susquehanna, then threaten Philadelphia, Baltimore, or Washington, and shortly thereafter, with luck, put an end to the war. The same optimism encouraged him to believe that Maryland was ripe for revolt. He said as much to Jefferson Davis, who agreed. All that was needed, they assured each other, was a little aid from Southern soldiers. Fording the Potomac, Lee's Army of Northern Virginia marched confidently into Maryland while the bands mingled strains of "Maryland! My Maryland!" with those of "Dixie." The first city Lee's men entered was Frederick. Bradley Johnson issued a proclamation to the people of Maryland, telling them that "the victorious army of the South brings freedom to your doors" but adding that "you must now do your part." [5] Lee issued his own proclamation as well. It listed the violations of civil rights suffered by Marylanders, including the arrest of members of the legislature, and assured them that the "people of the South have long wished to aid you in throwing off this foreign yoke." [6]

These Southern assurances got slight response. There were too many Unionists living in Frederick and the hoped-for uprising throughout Maryland failed to begin. In fact Scharf figured out that the deserters from Lee's army outnumbered the recruits from Maryland. Nevertheless Lee moved briskly toward Hagerstown after detaching a force under "Stonewall" Jackson to dislodge Federal troops from Harper's Ferry. Meanwhile the controversial Northern general, George McClellan, was following Lee. There was a brief battle at South Mountain, on the way to Hagerstown, and then the bloodbath at Antietam.

Wallis's clippings are replete with eyewitness accounts. Ob-

5. Scharf, *History of Western Maryland*, p. 230.
6. Scharf, *History of Western Maryland*, p. 231.

servers reported that some 200,000 men fought in the battle, which peaked on September 17. Casualties numbered more than 23,000, making it the bloodiest day our continent had ever seen. The *New York Tribune* of September 19 ranked Antietam as the "greatest fight since Waterloo." In the long *Tribune* story one brief episode could typify the rest. That was when Gen. George Meade and his Pennsylvanians pursued some of the Rebels into a woods north of Sharpsburg: "But out of those gloomy woods came, suddenly and heavily, terrible volleys—volleys which smote and bent and broke, in a moment, that eager front, and hurled them swiftly back for half the distance they had won." Antietam's wounded were carried to schools, churches, and even private homes in Frederick and Washington counties. Lincoln himself went to visit some of them two weeks later. Meanwhile the *Tribune* and other Northern papers which Wallis clipped described the outcome exultantly if inaccurately with such headlines as "The Union Army Victorious." The *New York Herald* moved a step further from reality when it headlined on September 21 the "Reported Surrender of 'Stonewall' Jackson and the Entire Rebel Army." Yet these boastful Northern papers weren't all wrong. Lee and his troops turned around and tramped back into Virginia.

The second incursion came in the summer of 1863. It was a preliminary to the Battle of Gettysburg. Lee's Army of Northern Virginia began a march through the Shenandoah Valley, across the Potomac, and into Maryland. Gen. J. E. B. Stuart's cavalry fanned out as far northwest as Westminster and as far southeast as Pikesville, with much alarm resulting for Northern sympathizers. Then he joined Lee and on July 1 Lee's men met those of General Meade to start the three-day conflict which proved to be the turning point of the war. Though we don't have any newspaper clippings about it from Wallis, we have a grim little reminder among his papers, in the form of a memo to him from Lt. Clapham Murray about Company A, Second Maryland Infantry, C. S. A. It states that the company entered the battle with a strength of ninety-five muskets. It left the battle with twelve men answering roll call. He adds that the company never fought again.

On July 5 Lee led the Southern retreat toward Hagerstown and the Potomac. The river was too high to cross, so when he got there he had to wait a week. Meade might have clinched a victory then but he chose instead to march his troops in a different direction, toward Frederick; and the great battle was over.

The third and final incursion, in the summer of 1864, was a punishing one. Federal forces had rampaged through the Shenandoah Valley in Virginia, burning houses and destroying crops. The Confederates, under Gen. Jubal Early, grimly retaliated and then menaced Washington in the bargain. Their cavalry galloped across much of Maryland; their infantry marched and countermarched. In mid-July the *Washington Chronicle* could report excitedly that the Rebels had plundered "the whole state of Maryland." They hadn't, quite. But they had battered and burned some houses, among them that of Lincoln's postmaster general, Montgomery Blair, in Silver Spring. They'd destroyed some crops. They'd made off with a good many horses along with an occasional wagon. They'd outfitted themselves—"ragged rebels" that one paper called them—at Maryland's expense. And they'd held several towns for ransom. Two cases were noteworthy.

Hagerstown was the first. Early's subordinate, Gen. John McCausland, described by the agitated *Chronicle* as "a fierce, middle-sized man with red, bushy whiskers," rode into Hagerstown on July 6 with about 1,500 cavalrymen. Threatening to burn the place to a cinder he demanded and got $20,000; he contemptuously refused to take it in Confederate currency. He also demanded more clothing than Hagerstown could give without going naked. He wanted 1,500 pairs of shoes, socks, and drawers. He got far less, some of it reminiscent of a rummage sale.

The second case was Frederick, a far richer target. The threat the Confederates made on entering was the same: pay ransom or see your community burnt down. But the sum was much larger, $200,000 in greenbacks. It was paid and some food supplies were also extorted. Other smaller towns were likewise raided, as far apart as pretty little Williamsport and Rockville. Washington itself was endangered. Early's men got as close as Belts-

ville and Bladensburg on the northeast and Fort Stevens on the
north. Lincoln rode out to Fort Stevens from the White House to
witness a night attack by the Confederates. The attack was
repelled as were others. Federal forces streamed into the city
and dug in. The odds turned against Early so he withdrew.

For Washington and Maryland as well, the hostilities were
practically over. Though nobody could tell just when the end
would come, there was no doubt that the North had won and the
South had lost.

In the tense first week of April 1865 Gen. U. S. Grant occupied Richmond, the Confederate capital, and a wave of exul-
tation swept through the North. For Baltimore, as Scharf put it
evenly, "It was indeed the brightest epoch that ever befell our
city for those participating in the Union cause." [7] Joy was tumultuous if not universal; and, as often happened there, tinged
with the threat of violence. But the only fights were small ones.
The report of the occupation came to the newspaper offices by
telegraph and circulated swiftly. A cheering crowd of thousands
gathered in the center of the city. "Merchants quitted their
places of business, laborers threw down their instruments of
toil, shopping was neglected." [8] Squads of police were called
out along with detachments of Federal infantry to keep order, but
they had little to do but watch benignly. Church bells rang and
"the cannon roared their congratulations of Union thunder."
Baltimore Street was festooned from Broadway to Carey with
more bunting and flags than it had ever displayed before. Even
some secessionists, feeling the pressure of events, "gave to the
wind the bright colors" of the Stars and Stripes.

On the morning of Saturday, April 15, the city learned that
Lincoln had been assassinated. Despite a driving rain crowds
came out and milled around aimlessly. Mayor John Chapman
ordered all flags flown at half-mast. The same bells which had
pealed out at the triumph in Richmond now tolled the assassina-
tion. Although on Sunday the weather turned bright and spring-
like the city continued to be subdued. It was Easter; the

7. Scharf, *Chronicles of Baltimore*, p. 633.
8. Scharf, *Chronicles of Baltimore*, p. 633.

churches were crammed and the sermons were eulogies of Lincoln. People draped many buildings and homes with black bunting. By early evening, according to Monday's *Sun*, "the streets were completely deserted, and the city bore a solemn stillness." When the city council met on Monday afternoon Mayor Chapman issued a statement saying, "Mr. Lincoln has had no equal since the days of Washington in all those traits of character which adorn the human mind; his patriotism and devotion to the Union were only equalled by his Christian charity, kindly feelings, and forgiving disposition."

That John Wilkes Booth had been born in Maryland was hardly Maryland's fault, nor was the fact that he fled there after murdering Lincoln. But Lincoln's secretary of war, Edwin Stanton, sent out a bitter bulletin on the supposed shielders of Booth. It opened: "The counties of Prince Georges, Charles, and St. Marys have, during the whole war, been noted for hostility to the Government. . . . If he escapes, it will be owing to Rebel accomplices in that region." [9]

On the morning of April 21 Lincoln's funeral train arrived in Baltimore on its slow way west. A large military and civilian escort accompanied his body to the rotunda of the big Exchange building. There the long coffin, magnificent in black and silver, was opened for two hours while thousands of persons filed past. In the afternoon his body was escorted back to the depot and a little later the train was puffing toward Harrisburg.

16. Public Weal, Public Woe

The characters thronging the stage of Maryland politics throughout the last third of the century were a colorful lot. No brief account can do justice to their schemes and counterschemes, their clashes and cries, their grinning triumphs and sullen defeats. But we can make some sense out of this welter through focusing on three characters: a pair of ill-assorted but powerful political bosses standing side by side in the center of the stage and, at stage right, an ironic, indefatigable reformer combatting them both, an aristocrat who loved the battle.

9. Wallis clipping book, 4: 7; Wallis Collection, Peabody Library.

During the war and for a couple of years afterward the Unionists managed to stay on top in Maryland. But it was only with Federal help and that was withdrawn following the war. Moreover, they fought among themselves at the drop of a stovepipe hat. Consequently, by 1867 the Democrats regained not only their civil rights, which many had forfeited in the war, but control of the state. From then on till 1895, as Frank Kent wrote in *The Story of Maryland Politics,* the political history of the state was the history of the Democratic party.[1]

This was not true simply because the Democrats were more numerous than the opposition, though that obviously helped. And not because the Democrats were smarter or had more statesmanlike leaders—they didn't—but because they were more cunningly manipulated. For several years after the war the struggle for party control seesawed, but by the early 1870s the Democrats were dominated by a duo so adroit that no leader in either party, in or out of office, could compete with them. Freeman Rasin systematically took over the city of Baltimore and Arthur Gorman took over the rest of the state. Complementing one another, they kept command for a generation. For the country as a whole it was an era of boss rule but few bosses survived successfully as long as these two in Maryland. They doubtless profited by the example of Boss William M. Tweed of New York, who was jailed because of the grossness of his corruption and died in prison in 1878.

If Gorman wasn't born to politics he was certainly schooled in it from boyhood on. Starting life in Howard County in 1839, he went to Washington by the time he reached eleven. His father got him a job as a Senate page. According to his biographer, John Lambert, he ran senators' errands for five instructive years, worked his way up to messenger in the Senate post office, then was promoted to assistant postmaster. He stayed snugly in that slot while others were fighting the war and early

---

1. Frank Kent, *The Story of Maryland Politics: An Outline History of the Big Political Battles of the State from 1864 to 1910* (Baltimore: Thomas and Evans Printing Co., 1911), p. 210.

in President Andrew Johnson's administration became the Senate's postmaster.[2] In 1866, already a professional politician, he got the job of collector of internal revenue for Maryland's Fifth Congressional District. He stayed three years, till the new administration of President U. S. Grant turned the young Democrat out in favor of a hungry Republican.

By then Gorman was set in the physical and mental mold he occupied for the rest of his career. He was a stocky young fellow with regular features and icy blue eyes, who kept his face smooth-shaven in an era when nearly all men let their whiskers sprout. Except for an odd half-smile he allowed himself from time to time, he maintained an impassive expression which came not from lethargy but from remarkable self-discipline. His movements were quiet but decisive, with none of the gesticulating, backslapping abandon of many of his political peers. He dressed as a rule in ministerial black and he kept a distance psychologically from the voters even in his beginning days.

Shortly after he lost his collector's job he entered Maryland politics with Howard County as his base. He ran for the house of delegates. The county's farmers looked favorably on Democrats, especially homegrown ones, and he had no trouble getting in. Then he was on his way, traveling a long road which brought him, when he was in the United States Senate, within striking distance of the presidency itself.

Six years older than Gorman to the day, Rasin was born in Kent County on March 11, 1833, of an old Maryland family. His schooling was better than that of Gorman, who never even learned to spell. Young Rasin had two years in the preparatory classes at Washington College before his father moved the family to Baltimore in 1847. After a little more instruction in Baltimore, he went to work. He began as a bundle-boy in a large dry goods firm and soon became one of its leading salesmen. He saved his money and by 1864 operated a straw goods shop on North Charles. In politics he followed his father, a Know-

2. John Lambert, *Arthur Pue Gorman* (Baton Rouge: Louisiana State University Press, 1953), pp. 6–7.

Nothing, and in the late 1850s was apparently head of the Blood Tubs.[3]

After the Know-Nothings disintegrated he turned Democratic. His first public office came in 1867 with his election on the Democratic ticket as clerk of the court of common pleas. It was a cozy job. Though supported only by fees charged for licenses, the main ones were marriage licenses, for which there was naturally an unfailing demand. Rasin remained clerk for eighteen years, using the office as his base while he extended his acquaintanceship, ward by ward, throughout the city. He made a point of knowing everybody, and everybody's weaknesses. As a politician he was nearly as interested in the poor voter as in the rich. He perfected a personal organization—an underground of informers and secret agents, often in the opposition ranks—which furnished him with a steady stream of facts and gossip and augmented his power. He kept most of his information to himself. When he shared it, it was mainly by word of mouth; and he delayed taking action on it till the climactic moment. In many a political caucus everything waited till his messenger arrived with Rasin's dictum. He had the conspirator's aversion to acting in public. Significantly, according to Kent, he delivered only one stand-up political speech during his forty-year career.[4]

Pictures of him are rare; perhaps on purpose he left few traces. Pictures of Gorman are many though not various: with the passing of each year he simply looks more senatorial, more made of marble. The few glimpses we catch of Rasin show us a swarthy, thickset man with a large head. Pouchy-eyed, he wears a bulldog expression which isn't masked by his mustache and clipped beard. He looks hard. Yet he had an ebullience which Gorman lacked, and to go with it a thinner skin. After they gained power both men were subjected to unremitting attacks. Kent observed that Rasin "bitterly resented them, writhed under them, and violently denounced his enemies to his friends."[5]

3. Sister Mary Anne Dunn, "The Life of Isaac Freeman Rasin, Democratic Leader of Baltimore from 1870 to 1907" (Master's thesis, Catholic University, 1949), p. 5.
4. Kent, *Maryland Politics*, p. 183.
5. Kent, *Maryland Politics*, p. 17.

He had reason, for instance when an ex-ally named John Gill called him a "Black Beast" and sneered that a committee of vigilantes should be formed to drive him out of Maryland. But about Gorman, Kent commented, "The mountains of abuse and vilification heaped upon him in the long course of his political career left him unshaken and serene." [6] Yet not entirely. For it's recorded of him that he never forgot an injury and also that he suffered from a lifetime of neuralgic headaches, stemming perhaps from more than neuralgia.

The men met in Baltimore in 1870. Introduced at a political conference, they sized each other up over lunch at Barnum's Hotel. The next time Rasin saw the friend who had introduced them he said, "That fellow Gorman is no fool" and was told that Gorman had said the same about him. By the next year they were laying the foundation for the "Ring," the clique of political bosses which they went on to lead for decades.

The tale of Maryland politics during the Gorman-Rasin era is lurid. The pair raised corruption to a science. Their machine inaugurated new techniques while perfecting the old ones. Kent claimed that the Democrats introduced the buying and selling of votes in the election of 1871. "Prior to that time," he assured his readers, "such a thing as a man selling his vote or buying the vote of others was practically unknown." [7] Whatever they did, Gorman and Rasin found willing hands to help them after they consolidated their power. Kent may have been mistaken in saying that vote-selling started only in 1871, but he wasn't mistaken in concluding that during this era "the politics of Maryland became thoroughly steeped" in sin.

Sometimes, as the years passed, the Ring aroused enough opposition to force it to make concessions, in either personalities or political practices. Then Rasin would grin to his cronies that he had to "perfume" the next slate. With his wide acquaintanceship he never lacked prominent Baltimoreans ready to run for office and usually to let him pocket the patronage. Or he might, in conference with Gorman, modify a party platform or

6. Kent, *Maryland Politics*, p. 15.
7. Kent, *Maryland Politics*, p. 22.

let a spurt of reform legislation through. Generally he didn't need the perfume to attract voters; all he needed was control of the polling places. Andrews, in his *History of Maryland,* mentioned a remark often attributed to Rasin about the windows through which the ballots had to be passed, "Give me the window and I don't care who has the votes." [8] Gorman grew subtler in his methods than Rasin, as time went on, but no less effective. His Byzantine maneuverings in Annapolis became notorious.

On neither the city nor the state level did the Ring have much of a program, beyond the bare essentials designed to keep it in command. It didn't need to. Long after the Civil War Maryland wasn't issue-oriented except on the touchy question of voting rights for blacks, where the Democrats were fiercely against them and the Republicans uneasily for them. Otherwise the state's two major parties were not only largely indistinguishable but stable in that interesting condition. Marylanders were apt to prize political loyalty as such and that made for stability also. William Preston often spoke about his fidelity to the Democratic party. Teackle Wallis thought of himself as a party man though he often scorned his party's leadership.

A perpetual reformer, Wallis was appalled, challenged, and, way down deep (we can guess), delighted by the rise of the Ring. Once again, as he had in the 1850s, he gathered the like-minded around him and became their leader. Like the Ring the postwar reformers shunned substantive issues and focused on political procedures. The two main reforms they battled for again and again were those of elections and government appointments. They strove for the secret ballot, well aware of Rasin's boast about the window, and the honest conduct of elections. And they strove for civil service reform, for the merit system, well aware that Rasin and Gorman stood unshakable in their conviction that to the victor belonged all the spoils. "I am no civil-service reformer," Gorman once observed bluntly in the United States Senate; "I do not believe in the system." [9]

8. Andrews, *History of Maryland,* p. 586.
9. Quoted in Lambert, *Gorman,* p. 86.

The reform movement came of age in the state campaign of 1875, termed by Kent "the hottest, the most bitter, and the most memorable" in Maryland's political history. He says that the "most conspicuous figure in the fight, towering above and overshadowing his colleagues . . . was . . . Wallis." [10] Gorman, not yet a United States senator, was running for the state senate from Howard County. The state Democratic convention met at the Maryland Institute in July; it was the first convention he really controlled. He used all his stock of wiliness and will to push through his candidate for governor, walrus-mustached John Lee Carroll of his own county. Gorman left his opponents at the convention livid at his hickory-tough determination. Kent quoted one of them, R. R. Vandiver: "I have been a Democrat for twenty-five years. I have witnessed Know-Nothing rule in Baltimore city, but I have never seen anything to equal the spirit of oppression that exists here." [11]

Wallis stood ready to welcome Vandiver and other disgruntled Democrats as, in a compromise with party regularity, "Independent Democrats." With his associates Wallis labored to form a coalition which would appeal both to the independent Democrats and to reform-minded Republicans. The leaders organized public mass meetings and held a host of conferences. Wallis used print to influence the public more than ever before. In an open letter Wallis flayed his chief opponents. He charged that Carroll had been nominated by the lobbyists of the state for their own evil purposes. He dared to call the lobbyists by name. In a heated response Carroll—termed by Kent "a high-toned, high-spirited, honorable man"—threw back Wallis's charges, scorned him as a slanderer, and intimated that he was a coward. Having drawn blood, Wallis redoubled his attacks. [12]

He even let himself be put up for attorney general on the "Citizens' Reform Ticket" against Carroll's slatemate Charles Gwinn. So many Baltimore business and professional men joined the coalition that the Ring began to worry. Gorman and

10. Kent, *Maryland Politics*, p. 43.
11. Kent, *Maryland Politics*, p. 47.
12. Kent, *Maryland Politics*, p. 49.

Rasin agreed that they needed to do perfuming, so they tried tardily to add some civic leaders to their legislative ticket. For once they failed and they probably lost the election, but with tactics like those of the Know-Nothings they snatched it back. What happened to one Thomas Pierce was typical. He described it in the *American* of November 11: "I left my work at the mills at Canton, and went to the first precinct of the first ward to vote. I had a Reform ticket. When I approached a short distance from the polls, I was assaulted by several roughs and handled pretty badly. My ticket was taken from me, and I was forced, against my own conscience, to vote for the Ring nominees." Officially Carroll won and Gwinn beat Wallis by 86,411 to 72,898. The votes the bosses didn't get by force they got by fraud. But the force and fraud were so flagrant that they helped to create a permanent opposition to Ring rule.

Vignette: Centennial 1876

So what else was new? The *Sun* on the Friday after the nation's 100th birthday was eager to inform us.

Leavening its front-page reports with a variety of ads, the paper observed that: The weather had been so hot that a tinsmith named John Sobboth, working on the roof of a house on Calhoun Street, was overcome and fell off the roof; however, he recovered enough to walk home. . . . A valuable mule belonging to the B. & O. Railroad was struck and killed by a freight car. . . . The massacre of General George Custer and his men at Little Big Horn two weeks ago was attracting much notice in Baltimore since some of his men had enlisted in this city. . . . The first of the new wheat crop was arriving from Maryland and Virginia; it looked fine and first-quality was selling at $1.50 a bushel. . . . Last night United Council No. 9, Junior Order United American Mechanics, paraded through several streets with music. . . . The harbor board met last night, Mayor Latrobe presiding, and awarded the contract for building the wharf at the foot of Hanover Street. . . . John Beck was fined $1 and costs for setting off firecrackers on the street. . . . William Winters was charged with stealing a horse and carriage worth

$400 from John Hartel of Gough Street. . . . George Smith, colored, was charged with stealing a coat, vest, and time book from John McCleary, value $10. . . .

And the assorted ads proclaimed that: The new Central Theater was scheduling a benefit performance of *The Two Orphans* for the actor George W. Thompson, prices as usual, 10 cents and 25 cents. . . . Tomorrow's baseball game at Newington Park would pit the Pastimes against the Ivanhoes. . . . The thirsty denizen or delicate invalid could buy the best of ice-cold soda at Habliston's Pharmacy. . . . The Odorless Excavating Apparatus Company would empty out your privy without offense. . . . The finest restorative in the world was Liebig's Liquid Extract of Beef and Tonic Invigorator. . . . Durang's Rheumatic Remedy, for gout and neuralgia as well as rheumatism, was being sold at all drugstores. . . . And Dr. Painter on Fayette Street would treat men's bunions while Mrs. Painter would treat women's.

17. Great Men and Nutmegs

Rasin extended his influence horizontally, so to speak; Gorman extended his vertically. In January 1880 Gorman had himself made United States senator. In those days, by congressional mandate, state legislatures elected most senators. Thanks to his practiced craftiness he received an overwhelming majority from both houses in Annapolis. We can imagine that it was with deep if carefully concealed satisfaction that he returned to Washington after fifteen years.

On Capitol Hill he soon proved to be expert in cloakroom politics. The sharp, observant boy doubtless had learned many things he could use as a man. Throughout Gorman's controversial career more than one observer came to that conclusion. A generation later, in fact a few weeks before Gorman's death, the muckraker David Graham Phillips published a magazine article accusing Gorman of corruption in the Senate; he charged that it was as a Senate page that Gorman had learned all the "crafty, treacherous ways of smothering, of emasculating, of perverting legislation." [1] Regardless, he developed an influence in the Senate, especially with the conservative southern senators, exceptional for a new member. Perhaps it was easier for him because they recognized that both his sympathies and those of many of his constituents lay with the Democratic South. In evidence, in the same year that Gorman went to the Senate the Democratic candidate for president, Winfield Scott Hancock, got 93,706 votes in Maryland while the Republican who won the office, James Garfield, got 78,515.

In the next presidential election the nation went along with Maryland, for Gov. Grover Cleveland of New York defeated the scandal-stained Republican Sen. James G. Blaine of Maine. Gorman played a key role in Cleveland's success and his rise to national prominence was swift. After the Democratic convention in Chicago he was chosen chairman of the party's executive committee. In that post he directed the heated national campaign. Up to the end there was a chance that Cleveland would be tricked out of the election, but Gorman knew—and coped with—every devious device of the Republican party managers. Two weeks after the election he traveled back to Baltimore in triumph. His was the first carriage in a long, noisy Democratic parade that passed through streets thronged with cheering supporters.

For Gorman, though he couldn't know it then, this was the most satisfying occasion in his career. When he left Baltimore to return to Washington he discovered that he had less influence than he'd expected with the new president; Cleveland was far from the party regular that Gorman himself was. Yet he managed to snare a number of posts for faithful Maryland Democrats. Rasin after eighteen years as a court clerk was named "Naval Officer" of the port of Baltimore, in charge of customs; and others, loyal if less powerful, were also rewarded. Enough of them in fact to persuade Wallis and several other reform Democrats to call on President Cleveland, doubtless in their finest frock coats, to urge that their recommendations be considered as well.

---

1. David Graham Phillips, third article in a series, "The Treason of the Senate," *Cosmopolitan* 42 (1906): 4.

Gorman's influence expanded in the Senate if not in the White House. In his home state, however, he saw the threat of trouble, the proverbial tiny cloud on the horizon. To be re-elected in 1886 he had to arrange, with Rasin's aid, that Maryland voters would elect a Democratic assembly in 1885. His opponents welcomed the threat, with the result that in 1885 another bitter contest developed, called urbanely by Kent "a splendid fight, well conceived and teeming with excitement." It involved the city election first and then the statewide one. The opposition to the Ring now fused together as the "Citizens' Reform Association" with Wallis as chairman of the executive committee.

In Baltimore Rasin saw that both his and Gorman's enemies were multiplying, so he decided once again to perfume his ticket. As candidate for mayor he picked a stalwart of the reform movement, James Hodges, who had often and fervently denounced him in the past. To oppose Hodges the fusion forces picked Judge George William Brown, who had been the mayor, and a courageous one, at the time of the April 19 riot in Civil War days. On October 7 in a jammed meeting at the Concordia Opera House Wallis gave the speech nominating Brown with, wrote Kent, "fiery eloquence."

Despite the zeal of Wallis and the fusionists the perfume worked and numbers of Baltimore businessmen were persuaded to support Hodges. But Rasin was kept so busy that he turned over the lower levels of ward politics and vote-buying or -stealing to a porcine young politician, John Mahon, nicknamed "Sonny," who became his chief aid. When election day ended there were enough votes to elect Hodges although the margin, some 2,500, was the slimmest in years.

The core of the reform movement lay in Baltimore; and after the fusionists were edged out in the municipal election, they lost some of their fire. Their efforts in the statewide election proved to be perfunctory. The regular Democrats won by more than 20,000 and Gorman's seat in the Senate was safe. When the new assembly met he received every Democratic vote.

Deciding to conserve their energies and concentrate on their city, Wallis and his cohorts started the "Baltimore Reform League" in November after the state election. The league's aims, the *American* of November 14 reported, were to "secure fair elections and honest government and expose official misconduct." In 1885 also, he and another aristocratic radical, Charles Bonaparte, established a journal they christened the *Civil Service Reformer;* to it Wallis contributed some of his usual vigorous articles, though his invariably delicate health was worsening.

Back in the Senate Gorman was received by his colleagues with uniform respect if not always admiration; in spite of his lack of seniority they put him on the powerful Appropriations Committee. Whatever his reservations, he felt he had to endorse the new Democratic president. One pleasant result was that the *Sun,* which admired Cleveland, "suddenly," John Lambert wrote, "warmed towards Gorman. . . . In fact, it even launched an attack against his opponents." [2] When in 1887 the national Civil Service Reform League blasted the way politics were conducted in Maryland, the *Sun* replied sanctimoniously that even "New York and Massachusetts, with all their boasted reform, [were] not as pure in state or municipal administration as are Maryland and Baltimore." [3]

For many Marylanders the *Sun*'s support gave Gorman the final stamp of approval. But not for Wallis. One of the things which made him so redoubtable an opponent was his gift for painting his enemies as fools as well as knaves. Was the senior senator from Maryland now reckoned a great man? Wallis pointed out that the senator was all too fallible, a credulous fellow who wore a nutmeg on a string around his neck to ward off neuralgia. The *Sun* had solemnly reported that fact, and with a frosty smile Wallis expatiated on it in "Great Men and Nutmegs" in the *Civil Service Reformer* for September 1886. "The prescription," he remarked, "thus relieves the throbbing brain of our statesman and leaves it calm and steady for the duties of patriotism and virtue."

The campaigns of 1885 and their aftermath marked the final burst of Wallis's fire. By the end of the decade illness forced his

2. Lambert, *Gorman*, p. 133.
3. *Baltimore Sun*, February 21 (?), 1887.

withdrawal from the political wars. By then he was regarded with widespread, though not universal, respect and esteem. He died in April 1894 at seventy-seven and was buried from Saint Pauls. Because he'd been a dominating figure in the political, legal, and cultural life of the city and state, some of the eulogies were so lush that they would have brought a wry look to his face. Even some of his enemies could laud a dead lion.

If Rasin and Gorman gave a sigh of relief if couldn't have been a profound one, for they had other things to disturb them. Rasin sensed a spreading uneasiness in his bailiwick of Baltimore. And Gorman was doubtless still trying to recover from a damaging event, his abortive run for the presidency. What happened was that, after Cleveland lost the bruising election of 1888, some influential Democrats looked around for a more appealing candidate. More than one thought of Gorman, skillful, determined, a party regular. No one knows how much he was behind the preconvention Gorman boom of 1892. Regardless, the New York and Baltimore papers speculated in May and June about his strength. In mid-June the *New York World* reported that half a dozen senators, mostly southern, were pushing him. He traveled to the convention city, Chicago, in state in the private car of the vice-president of the B. & O. Once there, though, he refused to run against Cleveland. He didn't want to divide the party, he said piously. Cleveland won the nomination on the first ballot; Gorman in spite of his refusal received thirty-six and one-half votes.

After winning the election a distrustful Cleveland turned to Rasin in Baltimore rather than Gorman in the Senate when he wanted to talk about federal patronage for Maryland. Writing for instance to Rasin from the White House on December 11, 1894, in a letter printed by Kent, Cleveland wrote about one job-seeker, "Please let me know what you would think of his appointment." [4]

Gorman's split with Cleveland widened. The *Sun* no longer smiled on him. It had a personal as well as a political reason: he'd kept George Abell of the *Sun* from being offered the post

4. Kent, *Maryland Politics,* p. 57.

of secretary of the interior in Cleveland's new cabinet. The *Sun* showed more and more enmity toward Gorman. By autumn 1895, in an editorial of October 11, it was calling him a Judas. It cheered on the Independent Democrats and the Republicans, who were gathering fresh strength. The state election, in fall 1895, was catastrophic. Gorman worked in the campaign personally as he hadn't for years; in Baltimore Rasin sweated in order to deliver nearly 44,000 votes for the Ring candidate for governor, a prosperous merchant named John Hurst. Notwithstanding, the Republicans swept the state. Their candidate for governor amassed a plurality of nearly 19,000. On the heels of the election Rasin wrote Gorman dourly, "I fear the expense of the thing has just about commenced." [5]

The next two elections further damaged the Gorman-Rasin rule. The presidential campaign of 1896 made them both—and much of the Democratic party in Maryland—very uncomfortable. The Democratic candidate was William Jennings Bryan, a prairie populist who preached a gospel of unlimited coinage of silver and alienated many Marylanders. Bryan lost the state by 32,000 to Republican William McKinley. The Republicans also won in the state elections of fall 1897, though by a hair; when they met in Annapolis the following January they chose Louis McComas for Gorman's Senate seat. A sharp-nosed fellow, with a straggly mustache, McComas was a ex-congressman from Washington County with an unsavory reputation.

More signs of the new times followed, including the adoption by the Republican legislature in 1898 of an improved ballot, at the prompting of the Citizens' Reform League, and the direction that ballots should thereafter be printed at public and not party expense. However, the Republicans like the Unionists displayed little talent for staying in office. They wrangled and cheated— one politician derided another because he "would not stay bought"—and the Democrats began to edge back in. In 1902 they were able to return Gorman to the Senate, where he stayed till his death four years later.

Nevertheless the Ring began to fall to pieces under the re-

5. Lambert, *Gorman*, p. 251.

peated blows of the reformers. The relation between Rasin and Gorman, long a marriage of convenience, became embittered. Each decided that the other was betraying him. In *The Story of Maryland Politics* Kent has suggested that both were correct. By the time they died, Rasin in 1907, a year after Gorman, Maryland was in a new era. Some of the old political tricks still worked and Maryland's history of political corruption continued, but no new boss became as potent as Gorman or Rasin. Nor did any foe of bossism repeat Wallis's dynamic role.

Vignette: The Seal and the Resurgent Motto

"Men Act while Women Talk." Who said it? Daniel Dulany, man of the eighteenth century? Teackle Wallis, the congenital bachelor? William Preston, at his most sententious?

No, none of the above. This forthright sentiment is inscribed on our Great Seal of Maryland. We got rid of it for awhile but it contrived to come back in 1876. Even today the seal's sexist message is spread throughout the state from Port Tobacco to Oldtown. It's still stamped on official documents. It's painted on some fancy state furniture. It's set in bronze in more than one state building. The marvel is that outraged feminists haven't demolished the whole seal long ago. It's true that the original of the motto is in Italian: *Fatti Maschi, Parole Feminine*. But that's no excuse.

We know little about the first form of the seal because the seal itself disappeared in 1644 and no picture of it exists. But we know that the seal replacing it in 1648 was substantially the one we have now. Its reverse side (the side we use) showed the coat of arms of the second Lord Baltimore, with additions. The arms were quartered for the Calvert family and the Crossland family, from whom Lord Baltimore was descended on his mother's side. Supporting the arms on the seal were a farmer and a fisherman, both in rustic seventeenth-century dress. The first held a spade while the second dangled a limp fish from a string. All very Old World.

Decade followed decade and the seal stayed with us with only minor modifications. It even survived the American Revolution, for during the conflict Maryland had more interesting things to do than to design a new and democratic seal. It wasn't till 1794, according to Clayton Hall, our best source about the seal, that a new one was ordered.[1] It was ordered from a Philadelphia firm and was about what we'd expect. Out went feudalism, looking sadly over its shoulder. In came democracy, spitting on its hands and getting down to business. The new seal proved to be as tasteless as Philadelphia scrapple. It featured a tobacco barrel with leaf tobacco lying on top. Next to it stood a couple of sheaves of wheat and behind it sailed a ship. The new motto? "Industry the Means and Plenty the Result."

Even tolerant Maryland couldn't stand such a seal permanently, so modifications were quietly made from time to time. In 1854 the Calverts slid back onto the seal with their quartered arms; so did the farmer and fisherman. But "Men Act while Women Talk" didn't make it. Perhaps some formidable Maryland females said warningly, "Look, boys, . . ." and staved off the motto. However, a second substitute was as fatuous as the first. "Increase and Multiply." Understandably, in 1876 the assembly brought back the old Calvert motto. In Clayton Hall's eyes "the ancient arms of Maryland were finally restored in their integrity."[2]

Since 1876 that integrity has somehow survived. Attacks on it have either been ignored by our statesmen in Annapolis or turned aside with efforts at diplomacy. Some well-meaning males have suggested that the motto really means "Courage and Courtesy." Nonsense. It means what it says, unfortunately, and it says it everywhere in Maryland.

1. Clayton Hall, "The Great Seal of Maryland," Maryland Historical Society Fund Publication no. 23 (1886), p. 30.

2. Hall, "Seal," pp. 38–39.

6

The Age of Gilt

18. The Farm, the Factory, and the Poor

*H*AVING survived the Civil War, Maryland's economy tried shakily to get back to business as before. There wasn't a chance. Far-reaching changes, some initiated even prior to the war, were taking place. For Maryland the salient one during the last forty years of the nineteenth century was the extent to which the farms diminished and the factories spread. By 1880 the value of our manufactured goods was twice that of our farm products, though as late as 1900 there were still more Marylanders in farming than in manufacturing. Our self-image was still agricultural, as it had been for more than two centuries. But agriculture had leaned on slave labor, especially in southern Maryland, and after the opening of the war slavery collapsed as an institution.

In 1860 the value of the state's slaves, as Scharf calculated it in his *History of Maryland,* came to more than $35 million. His was a conservative estimate; others have suggested sums as high as $50 million. But by March 1862 a Prince Georges planter, Dr. John Bayne, could write Lincoln in outrage: "Slave labor is disappearing so rapidly that our lands must go untilled at least for the present year, and the farmers will be ruined. Hundreds [of slaves] and I may say thousands have absconded, and they meet with such ready ingress and protection within the lines of

149

the Army that we shall soon be depopulated of slavery." [1] By 1864 a group of slaves in Hagerstown were appraised at $5 a slave.[2] By the next year they would have been appraised at nothing.

The tobacco plantations in Prince Georges and the more southern counties were hardest hit. In fact the tobacco economy never recovered in full although a substantial number of ex-slaves stayed on to become either paid farmhands or tenant farmers. Agriculture as a whole diminished in more ways than one. In 1850 the average size of a Maryland farm of any sort was slightly more than 200 acres; by 1900 it was little more than half that. The old Holly Hill place near Friendship in Anne Arundel County had 500 acres at the start of the eighteenth century, 167 in 1839, 147 in 1849, and by the 1930s only 125 acres.[3] Unfortunately this reduction throughout the state didn't mean that unproductive big farms were being cut up into productive little ones.

Some of the national markets shrank also, for more than tobacco, particularly in the piedmont between the tidewater and Appalachia. The soil there couldn't compete with the rich, black loam being plowed in the Midwest. In the piedmont the chief crops continued to be corn and wheat. The sole advantage they had, when set beside the tall corn of Illinois or Iowa or the vast fields of wheat in the Kansas flatlands, was their closeness to East Coast markets. But that didn't help enough, since foodstuffs like wheat could be shipped over long distances on the expanding railroad network.

On the other hand, for vegetables and fruits proximity meant a great deal. The East Coast was becoming more populous, more urban, and more hungry. Accordingly a good part of Eastern Shore agriculture shifted to truck farming and then made

1. Letter, John Bayne to Abraham Lincoln, March 17, 1862; Bayne Papers, Maryland Historical Society. Used with permission from the Bayne Papers, Ms. 1200.

2. Richard Duncan, "The Era of the Civil War," *Maryland: A History 1632–1974*, ed. Richard Walsh and William Lloyd Fox (Baltimore: Maryland Historical Society, 1974), p. 370.

3. Letter, Brice Clagett to Bode, September 26, 1976, and letter from Archivist Phebe Jacobsen, Maryland Hall of Records, to Bode, November 12, 1976.

money. The truck farms were served, directly and indirectly, not only by such major lines as the Pennsylvania and the B. & O. but also by such little, long-forgotten ones as the Philadelphia, Wilmington & Baltimore and the Baltimore & Potomac. They swiftly carried the vegetables and fruits from the farms and—no small item—the seafood from the Chesapeake to the cities: to Baltimore, Philadelphia, New York, and even Boston. Whatever couldn't be sold fresh was consigned to the tin can, and canning developed into one of Baltimore's prime industries.

Notwithstanding, Maryland's agriculture cried for help and Maryland's leaders listened. Among the aids they proposed was an advertising campaign. Precisely two centuries after George Alsop published Maryland's first promotional gem, *A Character of the Province of Maryland,* they commissioned James Higgins of the Maryland Agricultural College to supply a second. In February 1867 the house of delegates ordered 10,000 copies of his pamphlet published. It was entitled *A Succinct Exposition of the Industrial Resources and Agricultural Advantages of the State of Maryland.* The title, though, was misleading; there's far less on industry than agriculture.

Maryland is still the Garden of Eden; there's only a shadowy machine in Higgins's Garden, and no serpent. The inhabitants are still good if not necessarily innocent. Volubly Higgins assures the reader that they're "persons of kindly feelings, accommodating dispositions, disposed to respect the rights of others, and willing to perform the thousand and one little acts of kindness which make the sum of a 'good neighbor.' " They've even been decent to the Indians—Maryland's "colonial history shows no injustice to the aborigines." [4] The clincher is that Maryland as a Border state embodies the merits of both the North and South and avoids the defects of either.

Higgins's aim, however, differed from Alsop's. Alsop had wanted to attract the poor; Higgins wanted to attract the rich. He

4. James Higgins, *A Succinct Exposition of the Industrial Resources and Agricultural Advantages of the State of Maryland* (Annapolis: Senate Document, February 21, 1867), p. 9.

hoped to entice affluent settlers and investors to the state, particularly to the suffering tidewater region. So in his pamphlet he shrewdly reads the roll of the vegetables guaranteed to flourish in the tidewater's fields: onions, cabbages, peas, carrots, parsnips, tomatoes, asparagus, turnips, cauliflower, egg plant, oyster plant, beans, peppers, and both Irish and sweet potatoes "of great excellence." He also lists the fruits, all sure to ripen tastily: apples, peaches, pears, apricots, nectarines, strawberries, grapes, plums, figs, and pomegranates. The apples, for instance, are so splendid that Daniel Webster on seeing a basket of them thought them artificial, too beautiful to be true.

Still not out of breath Higgins proceeds to praise the varieties of Maryland seafood, "which exceed in quantity as they do in excellence all the rest of the United States." He comes to a climax, appropriately, with the diamondback terrapin, "wonderfully esteemed by epicures, and yet so delicate and easily digested that the daintiest invalid need fear [no] ill consequences from a hearty meal." [5]

Transportation for the products of Maryland's soil and sea is good now and promises to be better. The Baltimore & Potomac Railroad has already contracted for trackage between Baltimore and Washington. The Chesapeake & Delaware steamboat canal already offers "every facility for the transportation to Philadelphia and New York of the fruits and vegetables."

It's plain that Higgins loved the country more than the town. He readily and rightly concentrated on it, for the town was faring better than the country.

Throughout Maryland industry was on the upswing. In truth the whole nation was becoming industrialized and smoke plumed from countless factory chimneys. In Maryland the federal census for 1860 found some 3,000 factories large and small, with a total capital of some $23 million. The federal census for 1890 gave the number of factories as nearly 7,500 and the total capital as $120 million. In 1860 the labor force of about 29,000 created a product valued at about $42 million. In 1890 the labor force had ballooned to 98,000 and the product

5. Higgins, *Exposition*, p. 27.

was now valued at $172 million. On the other hand this wasn't the Gold Rush, Chesapeake-style: Maryland's growth rate was about the national average. The industrial center continued to be Baltimore. It dramatically outstripped the rest of the state, and the gap grew between it and the smaller cities of Hagerstown, Frederick, and Cumberland. Its population increased from 267,000 in 1870 and 332,000 in 1880 to 434,000 in 1890. Throughout that period the proportion of blacks was between one-sixth and one-seventh.

Nearly all the city's workers, white or black, made their living in one of three areas: manufacturing and mechanical industries, trade and transportation, and personal and professional services. Understandably, employment figures rose in all three. The census of 1880, for example, counted 50,000 persons in the manufacturing and mechanical industries, 32,000 in trade and transportation, and 47,000 in personal and professional services. Though there was no black-white breakdown we can assume from our other sources that the blacks were laboring at the least skilled occupations and, even then, were being pushed out by the aggressive white newcomers.

The fact is that more migrants than ever were funneling into Baltimore. The biggest group was native American. It can be broken down by race; it was more than two-thirds white and the total number of whites coming in between 1870 and 1900 was more than 80,000. Nearly 57,000 of them hailed from other parts of Maryland. Of the 35,000 blacks who moved to Baltimore between 1870 and 1900, 22,000 came from within the state.

Foreign migration was smaller, adding only about 12,000 to the city's population between 1870 and 1900. Still, ethnic patterns were developing. Already a city of native American neighborhoods, Baltimore was becoming one of immigrant ethnic groups as well. The Germans stood out. In 1880, according to the census, they were 60 percent of the foreign born and 59 percent in 1890. In token of their number, they were greeted when they disembarked at Locust Point with railroad signs in German as well as English. The Irish were 25 percent in 1880 and 19 percent in 1890. Trailing behind were the British, Russian, Austrian, and Polish immigrants, who averaged roughly 5 percent each.

Blessed by a constantly renewed source of cheap labor, with blacks ready to take up any slack the whites left, capitalism flourished in Baltimore like the green bay tree. Manufactures, sales, and services enjoyed a boom. The value of the investment in them soared from $38 million in 1880 to $93 million in 1890. Wages didn't show that rise; they barely doubled, while the buying power of the individual worker's pay actually shrank. Only one Baltimore family out of ten could own the place it lived in. The blue-collar class had to scramble to keep going. The middle class fared steadily better; its members were apt to put on weight. Its ranks were swelled by the liveliest and luckiest persons in the blue-collar class, who might if very lively and lucky exchange their few rooms for a row house. And the upper class: the canning magnates, the clothing manufacturers, the sugar refiners, the flour millers, the iron masters? They and their landholding peers tasted the joys of plenty. For them it was a Solid Gold, not a Gilded, Age.

The social historian James Crooks has charged that the 1880s in particular brought rich dividends to the city's capitalists but little more than long hours to the workers. "Industrialization," he has written, "meant more factories and more jobs, but it also meant more sweatshops, industrial accidents, unemployment during slack seasons, and child labor." [6] It also meant more foreign immigrants and black and white migrants to jam into the city's tenements, tiny alley houses, and broken down row houses. All this was little better than slum housing and was located in such neighborhoods as Canton, Old Town, Locust Point, Hampden, and Woodberry. The housing customarily lacked "adequate light, ventilation, fresh water, or sewage facilities."

Reports of the time corroborate his charges about the way many workers were forced to exist. Take the canning factories. The census of 1880 put canning at the top of the list of the city's industries. The chief of the state's bureau of industrial statistics

6. James Crooks, "Maryland Progressivism," *Maryland: A History,* p. 591.

and information reported on one cannery midway in the decade: "Hundreds of busy workers can be seen seated on plank seats, raised a few inches from the ground, men, women, and children intermixed . . . swaying their bodies in unison with the rapid movements of their hands. Women, with their infants at the breast, nursing their offspring while hulling peas for their own living. Children, three years old and upward, training their tender fingers to the labor which is their share of the family toil. Mothers bring their whole families to the packing-house, and the baby often slumbers in the pea hulls while the older members work." [7] He added that the workers were of both races but mainly Bohemian whites.

Then there were the sweatshops, smaller but just as bad if not worse. The men's clothing industry ranked close to canning as one of Baltimore's major businesses. It regularly supplemented its factories with sweatshops. During the 1880s the persecution of the Jews in Russia and Poland brought thousands to Baltimore. When they arrived the factory owners helped some to exploit the rest. With a capital as low as $50 or $100 an enterprising immigrant could set up a sweatshop and employ his less-enterprising fellows. Each shop made only one kind of garment for the manufacturer: coat, pants, or vest. And each shop housed one or more teams made up of a sewing machine operator, a baster, a presser, and two or three young women who took off threads and stitched simple seams by hand. They were all paid on a meager piecework basis by the owner of the shop. Many of them never got quite enough to eat.

In 1894 some 200 shops were inspected and the result printed in the bureau of industrial statistics' report the next year. Here again is a bureau chief's observation: "The bulk of the places that fall within the category of sweatshops are to be found in the territory bounded by Lexington Street, Eastern Avenue, Caroline Street, and Jones' Falls, though there are a number of others in various sections of the city. The Hebrews are the most numerous of those engaged in the business, although Lithua-

---

7. *First Biennial Report of the Bureau of Industrial Statistics and Information of Maryland. 1884–1885* (Baltimore: Guggenheimer, Weil and Co., 1886), p. 60.

nians and Bohemians form no inconsiderable part of the number. The shops are usually in dwelling houses, in some of which special apartments have been prepared, notably by the coat tailors, and in these an effort has been made to admit as much light and air as possible and to avoid many of the discomforts of the business. In a majority of the places visited, however, a large number of persons of both sexes were found crowded into second storey and attic rooms, surrounded on all sides by piles of clippings from the garments upon which they are engaged. . . . In addition to the clippings lying about, which is true of all shops, in many of them are found all sorts of dirt and filth either in the room where the work is being carried on, or in the adjoining ones, and the halls and stairways are swarming with half-clothed children, the imprints of whose unclean hands are found everywhere. The only entrance to some of the shops is through a malodorous side alley filled with stagnant water and other filth; thence up a crooked stairway and dingy hall strewn with pots, pans, and other cooking utensils." [8]

Such conditions cried for relief, as did the wretchedness of the poor in general. Doubtless the poor benefited from individual acts of kindness, doubtless often repeated, by Baltimoreans who were better off. But systematic help was scant. Among the few giving it the foremost was a friend of Wallis, another son of the lawyer in whose office he finished his legal studies. The younger John Glenn was a merchant, wealthy and civic-minded. At the prompting of President Daniel Coit Gilman of the infant Johns Hopkins University a group of civic leaders, among them Glenn, founded the Charity Organization Society in 1881. Its aims were to do good to the poor and do it efficiently. That meant, to the founders, doing good to the deserving poor while giving the back of their hand to the undeserving. So its charity was offered only after an "investigation of each application for aid as to extent and genuineness of need, the prevention thereby of imposture, and the registration of all applicants at a central

8. *Third Annual Report of the Bureau of Industrial Statistics of Maryland. 1894* (Baltimore: Sun Book and Job Printing Office, 1895), p. 80.

office to do away with duplication.'' [9] The society's original leaders also proposed to study the reasons for being poor and then to deal with them through the newly devised methods of social science.

But it was dry work. During the first five years the society's sole achievement was the supporting of two minor if complementary institutions, the Provident Wood Yard and the Friendly Inn. If we were poor and homeless we could chop up some wood blocks at the yard and then get a day's room and board at the inn. The society needed as much aid as the poor, if of a different kind. It got it when Glenn became chairman of the executive committee in 1886.

He showed himself to be full of ideas and eager to implement them. He soon set up a branch of the Provident Savings Bank, where the poor could drop their pennies—literally: they could deposit as little as five cents. He started the "Electric Sewing Machine Rooms," where poor women could be taught power-sewing. He arranged for university courses in charitable giving. He helped to start a journal called the *Charities Review*. By the end of the Gilded Age he'd strengthened and systematized the relief of the poor far beyond other reformers, and the effects were felt for years afterward. When the panic of 1893–1897 set in, the society stood ready. It helped to develop a Citizens' Central Relief Committee, of which its own expanded work-relief program was a part; it established Neighborhood Houses to bring its aid and social work closer to the poor; and it busied itself more than ever with measures, such as compulsory school attendance, which it hoped would prevent poverty rather than merely assuaging its effects.

However, because men like Glenn were few even on prosperous, bustling Charles Street, the condition of Baltimore's poor was drearier than now. Today we look back at their exploiters with a cold eye unless they chance to be our great-great-grandfathers. But that was the Gilded Age and the Gilded Age viewed them all, or nearly all, with innocent respect. It was widely held

9. Charles Hirschfeld, *Baltimore, 1870–1900: Studies in Social History* (Baltimore: Johns Hopkins Press, 1941), p. 139.

that the rich were rich and the poor were poor because God willed it. Scharf reflected this view. Half of his monumental *History of Baltimore,* issued in 1881, is biography laced with eulogy. Among the throng of rich men he celebrated we can't find a single freebooter. To judge by Scharf the Puritan ethic throve in Baltimore as it never did in Boston. He wrote for instance about the rich merchant W. T. Walters, who laid the foundation for today's Walters Gallery. He was "bold and aggressive, but cool and prudent; wide-reaching but exact; prompt to the moment in all engagements; holding his verbal promise in all things as of absolute obligation; never repining; instant in his intuition of character; a natural negotiator, but more a keen listener and looker than a talker; at work early and late; always on his feet; always coming out right in practical results." [10] How could a man like that sympathize with shiftlessness or deprivation?

Vignette: The *Hagerstown Almanac* for 1887

John Gruber couldn't have known how hardy a plant he was setting out, although he might have gotten a hint since he himself tended it for sixty years. A Pennsylvania Dutchman, he moved to Hagerstown, opened a print shop, and in 1797 issued the first *Hagerstown Almanac.* He both edited and printed it each year till his death in 1857. His heirs and successors had the wit to follow the pattern he'd established. For the first quarter of a century the *Almanac* appeared in German, though its contents from the beginning were aimed at Americans. Thereafter it appeared in both German and English till 1918, when the German version became one of the casualties of World War I. Its popularity proved to be as remarkable as its longevity. In the bottom of the depression of the 1930s it still sold 150,000 copies a year.[1]

Basically it's a calendar, and we can always use a calendar whether we live in town or in the country. But attached to the

10. Scharf, *History of Baltimore,* p. 677.

1. Writers' Program of the Work Projects Administration, *Maryland: A Guide to the Old Line State* (New York: Oxford University Press, 1940), p. 284.

Almanac's calendar is a good deal of astronomical and astrological data which must always have been pure mumbo jumbo for 99 percent of the *Almanac's* readers. The first calendar makers were astronomers and they left a permanent impress. Consequently, in the 1887 issue—to pick a representative one—we find lists of planets and their aspects, explanations of lunar characters such as the dragon's head and the dragon's tail, characters of the constellations with their symbols, and an astrological chart showing the part of the human body governed by each constellation. Plus astronomical calculations for every day of the year.[2]

Little though the calculations taught the typical reader, they provided the basis for the *Almanac's* chief venture: a gallant attempt to forecast the weather for each of the 365 days. However, Gruber and his successors weren't utterly reckless. They gave themselves an escape by printing the predictions, arranged by months, under the modest heading "Conjectures of the Weather." By the late 1930s the compilers of the *Maryland Guide* looked back and reported that the conjectures had been right about 60 percent of the time.[3] That was evidently good enough to satisfy rural customers throughout the decades, because they kept on buying the *Almanac*. And weather was vital to them.

The *Almanac* also satisfied its urban customers. For them the weather wasn't vital. Nor was the mix of astronomy and astrology; the craze for astrology had not yet set in. Nevertheless, the 1887 *Almanac* could advertise that it was being sold in Baltimore, Philadelphia, Chambersburg, Pittsburgh, and even Cincinnati. In fact it was selling so well that imitators were springing up, as the *Almanac* noted testily more than once. But why? Even if we grant that calendars and weather forecasts are handy to have around, we need more to account for the *Almanac's* success.

It may well have been the reading matter, which filled every second page. For one thing it furnished a guide to conduct and

2. *Hagers-Town Town and Country Almanack, for the Year of Our Lord 1887* (Hagerstown: John Gruber, 1887).

3. Work Projects Administration, *Maryland: A Guide*, p. 284.

personal improvement, something Americans have been interested in to an extraordinary degree. The motto on the cover sets the tone: "By Industry We Thrive." Or, as the 1887 *Almanac* observes, turning it around, "Man must have occupation or be miserable." Similar observations, ranging from a succinct sentence to an anecdote several paragraphs long, are abundant. Among them: that we shouldn't get ready to leave our jobs before quitting time; that we should be not only industrious but kind—anyone who's "tasted the sweets" of helping others will never give them up; that we should never delay till tomorrow and so on; that we should write to our mothers, especially if we're boys away from home; and that we should practice gratitude, for ingratitude poisons the bosom harboring it.

This isn't all. There's counsel on how to live long: don't run to the medicine chest for every little ailment; rest on Sundays; go to church for peace of mind; partake of "innocent pleasure and wholesome recreation." There's advice on more mundane matters. The ladies are told to open their windows and let the sunshine in. The owners of household plants are warned not to water them too much and never to douse them with cold water or they won't bloom. There's a recipe for fruitcake and a sure cure for chicken cholera: a lump of butter. There are tales with a moral and tales without. There are educational items, like one on the source of salt.

Doubtless this sounds deadly. Yet it wasn't. In general the *Almanac's* style was crisp and leavened with humor. Also, its editors knew how to tell a good story. The reading matter probably helped to sell the *Almanac* as much as anything—except the price: only a thin dime, a real bargain.

19. The Best of the Rich

Despite the indifference of the rank-and-file rich this was an era when philanthropy bloomed in Baltimore. Thanks to plans laid both before and during the Gilded Age by a trio of farseeing philanthropists, the quality of the city's life was permanently enhanced; they smiled on Baltimore and Baltimore has been the better for it ever since—and not only Baltimore. Quite properly their names have become household words. They were George Peabody, 1795–1869; Johns Hopkins, 1795–1873; and Enoch Pratt, 1808–1896.

Peabody had the kind of career which gladdened Horatio Alger. Born of poor parents in a Massachusetts town, he started working at the age of eleven in a grocery store. Then he clerked in a couple of dry goods stores including one owned by his uncle in the District of Columbia. At nineteen he set up his own firm there, then moved it to Baltimore in 1815. To build up his business he cultivated the transatlantic trade. He became a banker as well as a merchant. In 1836 he moved the main office of his firm to London, leaving a branch in Baltimore. By then he was rich. In 1843 he sold his business and concentrated on international banking. He grew richer still and began his handsome benefactions in the 1850s. They aided England as well as America. His character, like his benefactions, impressed British and Americans alike, and Queen Victoria regretted that because he remained an American she couldn't knight him.

In the late 1850s he laid the plans for the Peabody Institute in Baltimore. It was to have a library—"well furnished in every department of knowledge," he announced—along with an academy of music, an art gallery, and a lecture department. The Civil War interrupted the development of the institute but it went ahead after the war. He'd already contributed $1,240,000 and it was known that he planned to leave more in his will. The work advanced by stages. When the institute building opened in 1866 he stood on the steps, according to Scharf, while "before him passed in double file, with bright and smiling faces, more than twenty thousand children of all ages, from the tottering infant of four to the full-grown youth and maiden." [1] "A proud and happy day," Scharf concluded, "in the life of a great and good man."

The splendid library was the first thing to be put into operation, opening immediately after the proud and happy day. Its main hall was like an atrium roofed over with glass; it had five levels of balconies, all fenced with the elegant ironwork for

1. Scharf, *History of Baltimore*, p. 664.

which Baltimore was already noted. Each level was filled with stack after stack of books, a tribute to the librarians who had built up the collections. The conservatory opened in 1868, for the instruction of pupils, the giving of symphony concerts, and the presentation of musical lectures. The art gallery opened in 1881 although its collections were still spotty. The institute soon became central to the city's cultural life and steadily expanded its activities.

Peabody, said one acute observer who summed him up, believed that education, worthwhile jobs, "cultivated tastes, [and] the study and the love of art and science [were] next to religion, the great safeguards and purifiers of society, and accordingly he founded institutes, libraries, professorships, boards of education, to diffuse and encourage them among his countrymen. In all this, he followed the bent of his life—investing instead of spending." The observer was Teackle Wallis.[2]

Johns Hopkins began as a bookkeeper in his uncle's counting room, made some money as a merchant, and then branched out in classic capitalist fashion. Scharf has described Hopkins's progress: "In middle life he became president of the Merchants' Bank of Baltimore; was also a director in seven other banks, and was a manager of many other financial associations. He made large investments in real estate and constructed many warehouses." [3] Elected a director of the B. & O. Railroad, he took a busy part in its affairs and twice rescued it in a crisis. He never married and toward the end of his life gave a good deal of thought to how to use his millions.

In August 1867 he got twelve of his fellow citizens to form a corporation called "The Johns Hopkins University for the Promotion of Education in Maryland." In addition he asked nine of the twelve trustees to form the board of "The Johns Hopkins Hospital." Perhaps because of his own shaky health he showed a special interest in the developing plans for the hospital. He began making donations before his death to the two embryo in-

2. Wallis, "Discourse on the Life and Character of George Peabody, Delivered in the Hall of the Peabody Institute," 1870; *Writings*, 1: 87.

3. Scharf, *History of Baltimore*, p. 231.

stitutions, the most notable being thirteen acres of Baltimore real estate as a site for the hospital. At his death in December 1873 he left about $7 million in property and securities to it and the university.

The results turned out to be gratifying indeed. One reason Hopkins made millions was that he had a keen eye for ability. So did his trustees, for they recruited as the first president of the university Daniel Coit Gilman. In his essay "Self-Reliance" Emerson had written that an institution was the lengthened shadow of one man. For the university he was entirely right and for the hospital at least partly so. Debra Shore has described the man in a delightful piece in the *Johns Hopkins Magazine* for May 1976.

In mid-nineteenth century America Gilman was that rarity, according to Shore, a professional educational administrator. His scope was so broad and his educational interests so various that they sometimes made him suspect. A Connecticut Yankee and Yale graduate, he served at Yale as both librarian and professor. His lively mind was soon much appreciated off the Yale campus. Wisconsin and California each offered him the presidency of its state university; though he said no, he found the New Haven air stuffier than before. When in 1871 Yale needed a new president, Gilman was there but the Yale Corporation picked a pious philosopher instead. The University of California beckoned again. This time he said yes and was inaugurated in November 1872.

His stay in California was brief, interesting, and frustrating. He wanted a community of scholars, but the California farmers who led the opposition to him wanted something much more useful to the land. Not philosophy but agronomy. When the Hopkins trustees went president-hunting they found Gilman available. He crossed the country in December 1874 to confer with them and then, knowing that nothing was secret in a university, telegraphed the news of his acceptance to his daughters in Berkeley by wiring "Chesapeake Bay oysters have a very fine flavor." [4] He was formally installed on February 22, 1876,

4. Debra Shore, "The Launching of a Love Affair: Daniel Coit Gilman and the American University," *Johns Hopkins Magazine* 27 (1976): 27.

to the sound of instrumental music from the Peabody orchestra and the Brahmin accents of President Charles W. Eliot of Harvard, who delivered a congratulatory address.

The situation he encountered was tailored to order. Hopkins's bequest was the most munificent given to an educational institution up to that time. It came without strings, without "political or ecclesiastical interferences," as Gilman phrased it in his letter of acceptance, with a glance back at both California and Yale.

He began recruiting the nucleus of his faculty. He ferreted out men with brilliant and often unorthodox minds, and when he found them he offered them money, freedom, and research resources. Then he looked for the brightest advanced students. To start them coming he offered to pay them to study—a breathtaking innovation. As Debra Shore put it: "After having gathered that stellar and erratic crew that was to be the first faculty at Johns Hopkins University—Rowland, Remsen, Sylvester, Gildersleeve, Martin, Morris—Daniel Gilman dropped his bombshell. . . . He announced the Hopkins Fellowships." [5] The pay was modest, $500 a year, but the opportunity was unique and inviting. From the outset the fellows included men marked for eminence. Among them in the first group: Herbert Baxter Adams, who became a distinguished historian; Josiah Royce, a post-Kantian idealist who became, after William James, the leading American philosopher of his time; and Walter Hines Page, who became a prominent magazine editor and ambassador.

Having laid the foundation Gilman built on it imaginatively. He sponsored the creation of a group of learned journals, devoted to the latest study and research. He persuaded Prof. J. J. Sylvester to establish the *American Journal of Mathematics* as a starter and then supported the development of other journals. He sponsored the first genuine university press still in operation, the Johns Hopkins Press. He sponsored the development of seminars, small groups of advanced students brought together

5. Shore, "Gilman," p. 28.

for training in research by their professors. Basil Gildersleeve's held its initial meeting as early as December 1876.

Gilman was determined that his scholars should have the finest resources. Equipment for his scientists could be bought quickly enough, although it was expensive; but the library that his humanists craved would take decades to build up. So—blessing George Peabody—he arranged for them to use the Peabody Library, that "cathedral of books" as someone called it, which already housed nearly 70,000 volumes.

All this was very well except that it showed an intellectual elitism which ran against the Maryland grain. The more so since Gilman had also announced that advanced students were more vital to the new university than beginning ones. And the advanced ones could come from all over. There was a real risk that Baltimore and Maryland would feel left out. So from the first he called on his resources as a politician. He swiftly opened the university to the public, in the main through lectures intended, he announced, to explain "the methods and principles on which we rely." During the first year of the university the public could listen to at least 200 lectures, among them, besides single lectures, courses by some of the giants in their field: James Russell Lowell, for instance, on Dante; William James on psychology; and Simon Newcomb on the history of astronomy. The university proffered its hand to the city.

Teackle Wallis approved, and it was important in the Baltimore of that time that he did. Invited by Gilman to make a speech at the university in 1883, he said in it, "What the university needs to make the most of itself—what the community needs to make to itself anything of the university—is downright, actual, daily co-operation on the part of our people." [6]

Gilman likewise cultivated other Baltimore leaders. He made a pleasant impression, with his folksy manner and white muttonchop whiskers. Watching him, the sardonic young historian J. Franklin Jameson commented that one of Gilman's com-

6. Wallis, "The Johns Hopkins University in Its Relations to Baltimore," *Writings,* 1: 232.

mencement addresses was "full of the usual taffy, flattered the Baltimoreans and lugged in religion to please them." [7] His success wasn't surprising to anyone close to university affairs, for he managed to get along even with the faculty prima donnas, of which Hopkins already had its quota. Although the faculty grew, it didn't become any more tractable. There's a group photo taken twenty-five years after Gilman's arrival; it hasn't a smiling face on it, and nearly forty faculty members are pictured. The great classicist Gildersleeve sits at Gilman's right. Bearded, bald, staring out stonily under gathered eyebrows, he typifies them all.

In January 1889 Gilman shouldered another weighty but this time temporary burden. The trustees asked him to serve as the first director of the emerging Johns Hopkins Hospital. He knew far less about hospitals than universities. But so did the trustees, and in consequence they had commissioned five of the country's ablest medical specialists on hospital matters to advise them. From them the trustees had received a manual of 350 pages containing more careful thought on what a hospital should be than anything ever assembled before. Because the buildings were nearly complete by this time and the operating plans ready, Gilman characteristically decided that his job was to enlist the best possible faculty; there had already been an impressive start.

Part of the result is pictured for us in John Singer Sargent's famous painting, *The Four Doctors*. Because Hopkins was a teaching hospital, those doctors were professors as well. W. H. Welch was the professor of pathology, William Halsted the professor of surgery, William Osler the professor of medicine, and Howard Kelly the professor of gynecology. Dressed in their academic robes they look as wise as Solomon or Socrates; Dr. Kelly even has his finger laid symbolically against his temple. Osler and Welch were already stars on the medical faculty; then Gilman added Halsted and Kelly, and the hospital was on its splendid way. Johns Hopkins could sleep well in his grave in Greenmount Cemetery.

7. Shore, "Gilman," p. 32.

Then there was feisty little Enoch Pratt. Richard Hart has written his biography with urbanity and wit, calling it *The Story of a Plain Man.* A nailmaker in his Massachusetts youth, according to Hart, he would climb down from his carriage to snatch up a stray horseshoe nail on Saratoga Street. The commodities he sold after coming to Baltimore in 1831 were no-nonsense ones: nails and horseshoes first and after that hardware and coal. He was always a churchgoer, Unitarian, New England style. He gave freely to the church and recruited some of his aides from his congregation. In 1848, when he was worth half a million dollars, he moved into a red-brick mansion he built in Mount Vernon Place. In 1855 he made his first European tour, bringing back many memories and several marble statues for the mansion. When the Civil War broke out he sided with the North, though he detested abolitionism, and made money from Union contracts, especially for horseshoes. For the next fifteen years he thought about founding a public library with his multiplying fortune. Not a college—that would be only for the rich—but a circulating library which all could use.

In January 1882 he wrote Mayor Ferdinand Latrobe and the city council offering them a central library building to cost $225,000, along with several branch libraries. And if the city could pay an annuity of $50,000 he would endow the library with another large sum. A sum so large that we'd expect him to round it off. He didn't, though: he offered $833,333.33 more. The offer was accepted; the main building went up. It was Romanesque in architecture, with plenty of marble inside. A single newel-post can give us a notion of the interior's opulence for it was, said a contemporary report, "a solid block of dove-colored marble" and from it rose "an elegant bronze gas fixture." Literature has seldom been as richly lighted.

Pratt favored the appointment of women to the staff of the new library. Women were steadier workers than men and besides they cost less. Once the library opened its fancy doors in January 1886, he was its best customer. Not that he borrowed books, but he entered the building daily and often stayed several hours. He must have been a dreadful busybody, for Hart put it at its kindest when he observed, "There was no detail too slight, no expenditure too trivial to escape his scrutiny." [8]

He managed to make the library a model. Andrew Carnegie, the famed founder of libraries, admitted, "Mr. Pratt was my pioneer." He observed further that no free library in the United States had been planned with as much wisdom as the Enoch Pratt. Its 37,000 users, as of 1888, were more valuable "to Baltimore, to the state, and to the country than all the inert, lazy, and hopelessly poor in the whole nation." [9] A decade after Pratt's death Carnegie sealed his approval of the Baltimore library with a gift of half a million dollars to put up twenty more branches.

To us the three philanthropists are benign shadows, but they were formidable figures to their contemporaries and attractive ones to each other. Peabody in his prime was a big, tall man with a slight stoop; although his nose and chin were heavy, his mouth looked sensitive. Hopkins carried a quizzical expression on his face; his features were large. Pratt stood only about five feet tall, with a substantial square head, blue eyes, and a look on his face which warned, "Don't tread on me." They were all acquainted. Hopkins and Pratt were drawn together in Civil War days through their loyalty to the Union and their lucrative business with Union armies. After Peabody established his institute Pratt became one of the trustees; later he served as treasurer. When Peabody visited Baltimore in 1867, Hopkins had an important dinner with him. There's little doubt that at the dinner Peabody's vision and enthusiasm were catching; the next day Hopkins made his munificent will, and within two months bills lay in the legislature to incorporate the university and hospital he hoped for.

20. Behind the Row House Door

Middle-class living: so much a part of Maryland history and yet so often overlooked, both because we take it for granted and

8. Richard Hart, *Enoch Pratt: The Story of a Plain Man* (Baltimore: Enoch Pratt Free Library, 1935), p. 64.

9. Andrew Carnegie, "Wealth" (1889), reprinted as "The Gospel of Wealth" in *The*

because its records get thrown out with the trash after a good housecleaning. Luckily we can find a family in the Gilded Age which saved nearly everything and was blessed with a son who preserved it all for posterity. "Sacred rubbish," he called it. The family was the Menckens of Hollins Street and the son was christened Henry Louis.

They were ethnic, as we say today, and their main stock, German, was Baltimore's best known. They weren't sealed-off ethnic, though. There was a bit of Scotch Irish in the blood and plenty of non-German associations. In fact the head of the family had been heard to denounce Germans as idiots. For long years the family lived in a representative red-brick row house with representative white marble steps and carried on a largely representative life. That life is mirrored in two mammoth scrapbooks in the Mencken collection at the Enoch Pratt Library, headed "August and Anna Mencken and their Children. Souvenirs." The souvenirs, so-called, range from rent receipts to cardboard ads for August's tobacco business, with pinup girls dimpling as they urge "Smoke Havana Rose—5¢ Cigar." The souvenirs were pasted in by H. L. Mencken himself; he even added occasional annotations. And a prefatory note saying that he included "a great many household bills, for they throw much light on the daily life of the family." So they do.

The first item in the first scrapbook is his parents' wedding certificate, adorned with doves, rings, roses, and a cornucopia spilling out grapes, apples, and plums—thereby hinting to August and Anna that they should be fruitful and multiply. The certificate attests that they married on November 11, 1879, August being twenty-five and Anna twenty-one. August paid the inevitable expenses of setting up housekeeping. He saved the bills, listing the amounts in a little leather book he carried. He bought a new suit for $50, a silk hat for $4.50. He bought bedroom, dining room, and parlor furniture, along with seventy-eight yards of carpeting. He bought knives, spoons (but no forks), a breadbox, a coffee pot, and a piece of zinc to set on

Gospel of Wealth, and Other Timely Essays in 1900 and again in 1962, ed. Edward C. Kirkland (Cambridge: Harvard University Press), p. 38.

the stove. As a local businessman he bought almost everything locally. The furniture came off the floor of Rosendale's on Fayette Street, the cutlery and kitchen items from Robinson's on West Baltimore, and the carpeting from Mendel's, a stone's throw from Robinson's.

Food, clothing, and shelter: the three essentials. The scrapbooks tell us a good deal about what they meant for August and Anna though they certainly don't tell us all. About shelter the record is clear. August rented a decent enough row house at 380 Lexington for $16 a month. Because winter was approaching he bought coal and wood. About clothing the record is clear for August's main items, especially the new suit he bought each year. For Anna's clothing he either paid on delivery, or the dressmakers' and milliners' bills have been lost. About food the record is fragmentary. Very likely Anna paid for everyday groceries with paper money and small change, as most housewives did. At any rate the only bills to survive are for fancy groceries, though it's true they weren't very fancy—mustard and salad dressing, for instance.

For Americans there was already a fourth essential, transportation. Even this soon August felt he had to have the Gilded Age equivalent of a compact car. He owned a small buggy and a plug horse; the bills for hay and oats start in the first pages of the first scrapbook.

However, he was far from overextending himself. When he and his younger brother started their cigar business in 1875, it was capitalized at the breathtaking sum of $35. But it grew briskly because of August's good management. In 1882 he was considered enough of a rising young fellow to be invited to join the Masons. And in 1883 he could take not a step but a leap ahead, for he bought the newly built row house at 1524 Hollins Street which became the family's permanent home. As the family expanded its horizons, expenses rose. Among the first additional bills were those for taxes. The city charged August $63.53 in 1884 and the state demanded $6.58. Many bills increased because the family did. Henry arrived in 1880, his brother Charlie in 1882, Gertrude in 1886, and August, Jr., in 1889.

August's business grew as much as his family, one index being the cost of both his business entertaining and his social. His liquor bills mounted. But it wasn't only with others in mind that August stocked up on whiskey and beer. For the first Christmas at Hollins Street he bought a whole gallon of Monticello rye for $4. He liked the taste and tasting developed into a habit. His snooping little son remarked about it in one of his books of recollections. "Before every meal, including breakfast, he ducked into the cupboard in the dining room and poured out a substantial hooker of rye, and when he emerged he was always sucking in a great whiff of air to cool off his tonsils." [1] Not that August was prejudiced against beer; he ordered some each week. Although his favorite was Anheuser-Busch he experimented with other good brands. But for visiting repairmen, cellar inspectors, and other artisans, he thriftily laid in a grade D beer retailing at $1.20 for a case of twenty-four bottles. A nickel a bottle!

In 1885 August had some improvements put in the house though he had owned it only two years. And he continued to have it improved. There was already indoor plumbing for the family but only outdoor for any servant girls—they soon had at least one of them—and visiting workmen. That's why we see the bills for a time of the Odorless Excavating Apparatus Company for removing from the Mencken privy what's politely called nightsoil and masking the odor by burning buckets of rosin and tar. But by the early nineties August was asking for a bid from his friendly neighborhood plumber to replace the old toilet and add a new one. "I will furnish," R. Carruthers wrote in answer, "two flush-rim oval Hopper closets with iron tanks, all soil pipes, traps, and supply pipes for same." Furnish them he did, so that thereafter everyone went to the bathroom in style.

There were other signs of upward mobility. August ordered a shiny new buggy with a fringe on top and a new horse, a speedy trotter named John, to supplant his old plug. The buggy had to

1. H. L. Mencken, *Happy Days, 1880–1892* (New York: Alfred A. Knopf, 1940), p. 61.

be housed at night; John had to be stabled. Bills began coming from Reveille's stables and Miller's stables as regularly as our parking charges. Horseshoes were needed as often as we need tires, more often in fact. August got his from one S. Morrison, who advertised himself on his bills as a "practical" horse-shoer—not one of your dreamy blacksmiths with scrawny arms.

Middle-class life throughout Maryland ran more to buggies than to, say, Beethoven. Yet the scrapbooks prove that 1524 Hollins Street was no cultural desert. Like every sound Bal-timorean, August subscribed to the *Sun,* as early in his case as 1881, later adding the *Evening News.* By the time the boy Henry became addicted to reading, August had bought sets of Shakespeare, Dickens, George Eliot, and Mark Twain, along with such dogs and cats as *Adventures among the Cannibals* and *Peck's Bad Boy.* In the early 1890s he subscribed to Collier's *Once a Week.* It advertised itself as a magazine of "fiction, fact, sensation, wit, humor, news" and in 1892 claimed that, with a circulation of 250,000 copies, it was the most popular American weekly. He also subscribed to Collier's Library, which twice a month sent him a selected book. Anna had her own reading. She received *Godey's Lady's Book,* as she had even before her marriage, till it collapsed in 1898. She also took the much spunkier *Ladies' Home Journal,* with its crusades and drives, from the time it was first issued in 1883.

She enjoyed music of the sentimental sort, as well as reading. In 1888 August bought a square, black Stieff piano for her and the children. This was the piano young Mencken pounded, nourishing a love of music he never lost. When he grew up he especially enjoyed the compositions of the great German Ro-mantics, led by Beethoven, but his mother always preferred tearful popular songs. Her favorite subjects were female: dying maidens and abandoned mothers. Here's the first verse from the first of her song sheets which Henry pasted in the scrapbooks; it sets the tone. The young woman is entreating her beloved:

> Tell me you'll think of the happy past,
> Think of the joys we have seen—
> This one little promise keep for me,
> See that my grave's kept green.

Unlike reading and music, art meant little to the Menckens. The walls of 1524 Hollins were hung for the most part with somber steel engravings, among them a pair depicting the English seaports of Dover and Hastings, brightened by a few chromos like *Easter Dawn.* The scant statuary, judging from what we see in the scrapbooks, was made up of a Rogers group, *Fooling Grandpa,* and one "swinging figure," whatever that was. But the neighbors probably didn't have much more.

When we step outside the Mencken household and see its relation to the rest of Baltimore, we're struck again by its typicality. In this city of self-conscious neighborhoods and growing ethnic groups, the Menckens fitted in. Despite some reservations they kept their German ties. In point, they sent their children not to the public school but to Knapp's Institute. Though German had been dropped as the language of its classrooms by the time Henry enrolled, Prof. Friedrich Knapp was Teutonic to the core and so was the culture of his school. The first thing every morning, the school assembled to sing. Did it sing "The Star-Spangled Banner"? It sang "Fuchs, du hast die Gans gestohlen" or some similar Germanic jewel. In its drafty classrooms Henry got a feel for things Germanic and kept it. His writing was later sprinkled with German expressions and his Utopia was always a Munich beer garden. His father received good value for the tuition bills he paid and preserved.

The scrapbooks reflect a cheerful city, bustling except in the sultry heat of summer. True, a city pestered with annoyances we no longer know: insects (there were no window screens); major maladies such as typhoid fever, along with many minor ones; the stench from the accumulated sewage in the back basin of the Patapsco River. Yet a city full of optimism. Even the smell of the sewage, Mencken said, was supposed to toughen those forced to inhale it and let them live longer. The streets often looked attractive. People walked along them for recreation, stopping to chat with friends. The buggies bounced over the cobblestones and Belgian blocks noisily but not offensively. The street lamps were lit each evening by public lamplighters. Not that everything in Baltimore was sugar and spice but for many people like the Menckens the Gilded Age was a fine time to be a Baltimorean.

7

The Mencken Era and Beyond

21. Beer, Boom, and Bust

THE 1920s, our last great Age of Euphoria, arrived in Maryland carrying a hip flask, dancing the fox-trot, and dressing on credit. All at the same time.

Despite its gaudiness, the decade rested on a firm base of bourgeois virtues and living. They were taken for granted; they weren't newsworthy. But they were important. We can find them, as often as not, in Mencken. He was born in the Baltimore bourgeoisie and, despite his rise to international fame, stayed in it throughout his life. He spent all but five of his seventy-five years in the family row house. He had the appetites of a bourgeois: good, heavy food; good beer, fairly good whiskey and wine; and good company, preferably male. He had the values of a bourgeois: work before play; save for tomorrow; and, above all for him, keep engagements. He had the prejudices of a bourgeois, the prejudices others kept hidden but which he flaunted in his articles and books. He even had a classic bourgeois look, with his chubby face and chunky body in its sedate blue suit.

Besides being a bourgeois he was a local figure who identified with his locality. Though their defects made him wince he loved Baltimore and Maryland also, and published his love. "Good old Baltimore" he called the city. Moreover, he prized

174

the state as a whole, even if he had qualms about the Eastern Shore, with its insularity and unabashed racism. He thought that the prettiest part of Maryland was the piedmont, especially in Howard County where "fat cattle graze in the meadows, there are sheep upon most of the hills, and noble groves of well-kept trees break the monotony of the fields." [1]

On the other hand he was much more than a middle-class Marylander. Through his writing he became the national spokesman for the intellectuals of the 1920s because he formulated their feelings more tellingly than anyone else. These feelings were a paradoxical compound of disenchantment, defiance, and zest for living. The American experience, including that of intellectuals, is that we can be idealists only for a short span. There was an undeniable element of idealism in our entering World War I. We wished, as Woodrow Wilson claimed, to make the world safe for democracy. At home we paraded; we ate bran bread; we bought Liberty Bonds. An outspoken pro-German, Mencken ridiculed all this but he was in an unheeded minority till the twenties. Then disenchantment and defiance grew fashionable. We turned to our private concerns, searching for self-fulfillment and amusement. We were no longer interested in Holy Wars, not even in issues. We gazed vacantly at anyone mentioning the League of Nations or tariff reform, farm support, or disarmament.

But at the mention of Prohibition we sprang to life. The shrewdest political observer the state had, Frank Kent, pronounced it the only issue to galvanize the public, in or out of Maryland. What had happened was that some earnest Americans, using the same idealism that briefly made us want to save the world, had tried to save us from ourselves. They were the leaders in the temperance movement; their sinewy political arm was the Anti-Saloon League. The triumph over their official enemies, drunkenness and the saloon, was signaled by the Eighteenth Amendment to the Constitution. Maryland's general assembly ratified it in February 1918; it was adopted nationally by January 1919 and went into effect a year later.

1. Mencken, "Spring in these Parts," *Evening Sun*, April 12, 1926.

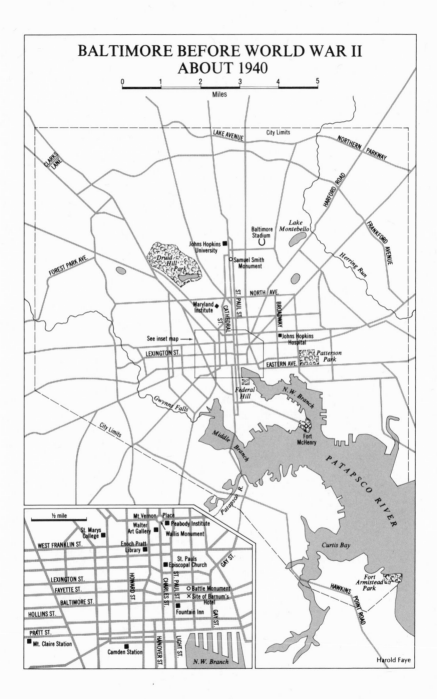

BALTIMORE BEFORE WORLD WAR II
ABOUT 1940

0   1   2   3   4   5
Miles

LAKE AVENUE   City Limits

NORTHERN PARKWAY

CLARKS LANE

HARFORD ROAD

FRANKFORD AVENUE

FOREST PARK AVE

Druid Hill Park

Johns Hopkins University

Baltimore Stadium

Lake Montebello

Herring Run

Samuel Smith Monument

ST. PAUL ST.

NORTH AVE.

Maryland Institute

CATHEDRAL ST.

BROADWAY

See inset map →

Johns Hopkins Hospital

LEXINGTON ST.

Patterson Park

EASTERN AVE.

Federal Hill

N.W. Branch

Gwynns Falls

City Limits

Middle Branch

Fort McHenry

Patapsco R.

PATAPSCO RIVER

Curtis Bay

Fort Armistead Park

HAWKINS POINT ROAD

½ mile

Mt. Vernon Place

Walter Art Gallery

Peabody Institute

Wallis Monument

St. Marys College

Enoch Pratt Library

WEST FRANKLIN ST.

St. Pauls Episcopal Church

GAY ST.

LEXINGTON ST.

FAYETTE ST.

BALTIMORE ST.

HOWARD ST.

CHARLES ST.

ST. PAUL ST.

Battle Monument

Site of Barnum's Hotel

Fountain Inn

GAY ST.

HOLLINS ST.

PRATT ST.

Mt. Claire Station

Camden Station

HANOVER ST.

LIGHT ST.

N.W. Branch

Harold Faye

The first, and key, section decreed that the "manufacture, sale, or transportation of intoxicating liquors . . . is hereby prohibited." Intoxicating meant having as little as .5 percent of alcohol. The beer that Mencken and his companions had always swigged contained 3 or 4 percent, the wine 10 to 15 percent, and the rye his father had relished, probably 40 percent. Roars of outrage soon resounded through much, if not all, of Maryland; season by season their volume rose. In December 1933 the Twenty-first Amendment repealed the Eighteenth. In between came what Mencken called in eye-rolling retrospect "The Thirteen Dreadful Years."

At the outset the presumption was that Prohibition would be enforceable and would "dry up" every state in the Union. But Maryland considered itself wetter than most states; in addition its newest and most magnetic leader stood boldly against enforcement. He was the libertarian Albert Cabell Ritchie. Dark-browed, silver-haired, attractive, he drew more support than any other politician of his day. An independent Democrat, he faced down the heirs of Gorman and Rasin with the result that in 1916, at forty, he was elected attorney general. In 1919 he squeaked in as governor and won re-election three times, by growing majorities. From 1920 to 1934 he ruled Maryland and spoke for the state. In a major address at a national conference of governors in 1922, he declared that Marylanders regarded Prohibition "as an unnecessary and drastic federal infringement on their state and personal rights."

In Maryland and elsewhere Prohibition became not only a law to be flouted but an excuse for a new, daring style of postwar life. It relaxed rules of conduct which the nation had long taken for its norms. To a country increasingly open about sex it brought a sexual revolution, especially for young women. Along with words like "bootlegger," "hijacker," and "speakeasy," words like "necking" and "petting" popped up in the American vocabulary. The movies, shaping our culture as well as reflecting it, showed close-ups on the silent screen of heaving bosoms and parted lips in bedrooms or rumble seats. At the opening of the decade Maryland's board of motion picture censors boasted that it had "kept the flood of salacious and pernicious films to a great extent out of the state." [2] The boast was hollow.

Defying Prohibition became a game, an adventure not without risks, and a crusade. A game that had as its object gulping down illegal liquor regularly even if it tasted to us, as did bathtub gin, like fiery violets. An adventure in that we risked arrest when buying or making liquor. And a crusade against the violation Ritchie had denounced of our personal rights. More than most states Maryland had built up a reputation for respecting personal freedoms, among them freedom of worship and freedom of speech. It took its reputation seriously. When in 1923 Hamilton Owens, editor of the *Evening Sun,* yeasty younger brother of the morning paper, coined the phrase "The Maryland Free State," it caught on at once. Mencken, who seldom took anything seriously, devoted an article to the origins of all this tolerance. He alleged that in Maryland opposites were so evenly balanced, mainly the Eastern Shore against the western one, that Maryland had either to learn forbearance or face extinction. Likewise in religion; he maintained that Catholics and Protestants were nearly enough matched so that if tempted to intolerance they could have destroyed each other.[3] That was a simplification but not a gross one.

True, this broad-mindedness hadn't developed without resistance. Baltimore itself, though he praised it in his article as a "factor making for tolerance," clung to a covert puritanism, especially in its subscribing along with the rest of the state to a code of "Blue Laws" which featured punishments for "Sabbath-Breaking." The laws forbade such activities on Sunday as working, bowling, fishing, and shopping except for a few miscellaneous items like cigarettes, candy, and milk. Regardless, respect for personal rights remained an ideal. To many thousands during the 1920s, freeing the state from Prohibition seemed an admirable and appropriate thing to do. Among their leaders was Mencken. Throughout the Thirteen Dreadful Years he fired his Roman candles at it with relish.

2. *Fifth Annual Report of the Maryland State Board of Motion Picture Censors, 1920–1921* (Baltimore: 1921?), p. 3.

3. Mencken, "Notes on the Free State," *Evening Sun,* February 21, 1926.

He attacked it at home, literally, as well as abroad. Like other Marylanders he concocted home brew. But he did it flamboyantly. As early as December 1920 we know he was at work, for he cried to his Detroit friend Harry Rickel for help: "Send me the name of the baker's malt man, in God's name. Down here they would sell me only a barrel—about 300 pounds." [4] And as late as March 1933 he wrote Rickel about his beer-making: "Last Sunday I manufactured five gallons of Methodistbräu. It turned out to be very tasty." [5] The only trouble was that he bottled it too soon, with fearful explosions resulting and bottles shattering across the cellar.

Abroad Mencken fought Prohibition mainly through many of his "Monday Articles" which adorned the *Evening Sun* editorial page from 1920 to 1938. During most of that time he ranked as the nation's liveliest journalist and the shiniest gem in the *Sunpapers'* diadem, so it was no surprise that he had the chance in these articles—from "Notes on the Drought," August 5, 1920, to "After the Deluge," April 10, 1933—to make Prohibition look either vastly villainous or ludicrous.

When it came to actions rather than words Mencken considered himself too decrepit to venture beyond beer-brewing. Instead he watched the Prohibition circus with a grin, along with the jazzy American Way emerging in the twenties. Each day he read the morning and evening *Sunpapers* as they reported news and views. He saw unrolled before him the world of Warren Harding and Calvin Coolidge, Reds and Red-baiting, hijackers and stick-up men, short hair and shortening skirts, Babe Ruth and Red Grange, and installment buying and business booms— and busts. When we read those papers today, they still give us a sense of the times. Often the headlines suffice to tell the story. We might pick a month in 1920, 1923, 1926, 1929, 1932, and 1935 to look at.

Suppose we riffle through the issues of the *Evening Sun* for January 1920, the start of the decade. Politics and crime, as

4. Letter to Harry Rickel, December 20 [1920]; *Letters of H. L. Mencken,* ed. Guy Forgue (New York: Alfred A. Knopf, 1961), p. 215.

5. Letter to Harry Rickel, March 27 [1933]; *The New Mencken Letters,* ed. Carl Bode (New York: Dial Press, 1977), p. 285.

always, are the staple of the news. Currently one story reports that, as its headline says, the "Cost of Government Continues to Mount." Another says that the drys are lobbying to make smoking as well as drinking illegal. Because the federal government considers Communists a menace: "Over 4500 Seized in Raids on Alleged Reds; 31 Arrested in Baltimore." The story explains that the government hopes to ship them all back to Russia and that the arrests were made in "a cool, systematic manner." Automobile thefts are occurring, even on the streets of Baltimore. We see from the news item on one that the term for it is "autojacking." "Hijacking" hasn't come into use yet, though the *Sun* reports an instance: "44 Cases of Liquor Stolen in Hold-Up." The top sports story is that Babe Ruth, Baltimore's own, has been sold to the New York Yankees by the Boston Red Sox for more than $100,000.

Advertisements lie scattered among the news stories. The prices they quote look enviably low to us, but they're high for the time and a headline advises us: "Cheer Up, Highest Prices to Come." Hecht's Furniture Stores coo, "Do it with credit in 1920." Hochschild, Kohn is selling gingham housedresses at $2.85; the Hub has an ad for young men's suits with modishly pinched waists at $29.50. Berkheimers has eggs at 58¢ a dozen, chickens at 39¢ a pound, and—a bargain—porterhouse steak at 30¢. Another kind of ad whispers confidentially, "He darkens his gray hair." And a full-page spread from the National Canners Association tells Baltimoreans "The Wonderful Story of the Tin Can." Who says business has lost its romance?

The issues of the morning *Sun* for September 1923 carry us further into contemporary life. Among the stories: the press club has held a memorial service for the late President Warren Harding, with Boy Scouts as ushers. His was "a religious character" according to one of the eulogists. The inference is that we'll miss leaders like Harding, for sin is rising all around us. One Sunday the Reverend Edward Taber addresses his congregation at the Hampden Methodist Church on "Booze-Soaked Baltimore," castigating Governor Ritchie in the process. Congressman John Philip Hill is defying the federal agents by making grape wine in his home on W. Franklin Street and taunting them with its rising alcoholic content; the *Sun* provides a running account. Other signs of the weakening of our ways include the case of Mrs. Charles Hobeck. She's reported as complaining to a magistrate in police court that her husband has acted mean ever since she took $2 he gave her to pay a bill and spent it on having her hair bobbed and curled. At the Century Pola Negri and Jack Holt are playing in a lusty movie, *The Cheat*. The *Sun* isn't itself averse to doing a bit of corrupting. It headlines one of its stories "Girl Who Bared Knee in Court Wins Verdict."

Ads entice the public as usual. For 75¢ we can buy a record of "No No Nora." For $11 we can buy a stylish-stout corset. For $24.50 a floor lamp with a fringed silk shade. And for $490 a new Chevrolet roadster. In fact some spoilsport claims that we're becoming auto-mad: "Says Many Skimp Food to Buy 'Gas.'" This seems hardly necessary since eggs, for instance, have dropped to 37¢ a dozen and potatoes are 16¢ a pound.

In 1926, the year of the sesquicentennial, we continue along the road to perdition. In June the *Sun* carries ads showing knee-length skirts. Men's wear is still sedate, however; Van Heusen advertises collars for 50¢ apiece. "Smartness and Comfort" is the Van Heusen slogan. Food prices are higher but they still leave us with enough cash to smoke if we like. And cigarette ads are growing larger and more alluring—among them a full-page invitation to have a Camel: "No cigaretty aftertaste." Radios are competing with movies for our leisure hours. If we don't want to watch seductive Pola Negri in *Social Highwayman*, we can dance the Charleston to our radio. Station WCAO advertises that its evening program presesents the dance music of the South Sea Rhythmatics. Or we can simply sit and read the "funnies." There are more comic strips in the *Sunpapers* all the time: "Mutt and Jeff," "Gasoline Alley," and a score of others. Moreover, they're still comic, with jokes, sight gags, and characters falling over backward at the punch line.

However, life isn't all froth. The Polytechnic Institute has just graduated a record class of 249 at its June commencement. Mayor Howard Jackson has assured the class that opportunities lie ahead for those who apply themselves.

Leafing through issues of the *Sun* of October 1929 can give us an odd sensation. We know that catastrophe waits at the end of the month. Emerson's Bromo-Seltzer advertises an offering of 56,000 shares to the public at $33 a share, and business for headache remedies is going to be brisk. Although the stock market is skittish—or as the *Sun* puts it on the 12th, "Highly Irregular"—nobody seems to pay attention. Prohibition is a more titillating topic; the *Sun* quotes the U.S. district attorney, Amos Woodcock, as saying morosely that the modern speakeasy is a "mean, pitiful place."

We're amusing ourselves in other ways besides defying the Eighteenth Amendment. Many Marylanders follow sports and a treat's waiting for them. Notre Dame will play Navy at the Baltimore Stadium, the peak game for football fans. Mayor William Broening, successor to Mayor Jackson, exhorts everyone to show "Football Spirit." We're listening to the radio more than ever. Radios are getting better and more costly. We can buy an Atwater-Kent for $136. Or an RCA Radiola Super-Hetrodyne at a price so high that the ad doesn't even include it, offering easy credit instead. At the movies the best bets seem to be Lenore Ulric in *Frozen Justice* (love up North) and Ann Harding in *Her Private Affair* (sophisticated dalliance). The cigarette ads remain frequent and one brand shows more daring than the rest: Old Gold pictures a woman actually holding a cigarette.

By the middle of the month the portents of disaster are plain but still unheeded. The *Sun* buries in its back pages a headline like "Wheat Collapses in Chicago Market" and threatening news like the stock plunge a few days later. On the 24th, however, the *Sun* runs a double-column front-page story on the stock market, headed "$3,000,000,000 Vanishes in One Hour," about a storm of distress selling. That's on Black Thursday. But if we think things can't possibly get worse, we know better on the 29th, Black Tuesday. It's a debacle that brings an end to more than a decade; it brings an end to an era. Our economic system will never be the same, nor will the vaunted American Way.

We can notice the difference when we look at the *Sun* during, for instance, October 1932. It's a bleak world now for the average family and the average business. The cities themselves are in trouble: "Bankers Balk at Loan to New York." Yet ordinary life continues somehow. The staples of the news continue to be politics and crime, though crime is less visible than we might expect in a period of want and dislocation. Politics, however, is making more headlines than usual, because this is the year for electing a president. Although the *Sun* stays conservative it has long ago given up on Herbert Hoover. "His Own Worst Enemy" it calls him in an editorial on the 15th. There's an ad the same day announcing "President Hoover on Air Tonight." The ad quotes Calvin Coolidge in a perfectly characteristic statement, "Things are much worse in other parts of the world." Governor Ritchie has gone to Northwestern University as a representative of the Democratic nominee, Franklin Delano Roosevelt, to debate a representative of Hoover. On November 8 Roosevelt wins by a landslide. In Maryland, the *Sun* reports, his total is 314,000 to Hoover's 184,000. A new day is coming.

It's overdue. Household Finance runs an ad showing a white-collar male bent over his desk with brows knitted. The caption is "Bills! Bills! Bills!" The depression is blighting almost every group, though the *Sunpapers* are obviously less affected than most businesses and have adopted the haughty habit of calling the jobless "The Idle." Still there's some money around and prices are low. A man can buy a new suit at Agee's with broad lapels and a vest for $17.50. A woman can buy a coat with a fur collar for $25.95. Food is cheap also. There are ads for chicken at 28¢ a pound and chuck roast at an unbelievable 13½¢.

Our search for relief from the bleakness of the depression is reflected here and there in the papers. Brand-new table radios are advertised for as little as $11.95, and tuning in has become a great American pastime. We can listen to stations all over the country or we can tune in on WCAO from morning (7:45, Snowball; "Laugh with this happy fellow") till late at night (semiclassical music). Given a little cash we can drop in at the movies, our premier escape, to see Joan Crawford in *Rain,* for example, or Marlene Dietrich in *I Kiss Your Hand, Madame.* Some of us play cards and the fashionable new game is contract bridge. The *Sun* is running a regular column on it by a "bridge master.'' A few of us have enough money and ambition to go to the recital at the Lyric by Lawrence Tibbett of the Metropolitan Opera, radio, and the ''singing movies.'' If we're in college we have other recreations: a news story of the 26th says that some students at Saint John's College in Annapolis have been charged by the police with ''making whoopee.''

Lastly we might scan the *Sun* for, say, February 1935, by which time the New Deal has not only begun but is ballooning. Government agencies at every level have been created to meet our myriad emergencies. They've all become known by their initials, causing many a quip about Washington's ''alphabet soup.'' The federal ones include, in the order of their creation: the FERA, the AAA, the HOLC, the NIRA, the CWA, the SEC, and the FHA. All these in only two years, 1933 and 1934. The local one mentioned in the *Sun* most often in February 1935 is BERC, the Baltimore Emergency Relief Commission. The attention it gets isn't surprising. The paper reports on the second that BERC has a load of nearly 30,000 welfare cases. A few days later there's an item about a man charged with defrauding BERC of $187.54 by hiding the fact that his wife has been working for $14 a week. The same day there's an announcement in the paper of the kind that drives Mencken and other conservatives up the fiscal wall. The U.S. Treasury confesses that it has received only 51¢ in taxes for every dollar the government has spent last year.

The variegated efforts of the New Deal are apparently doing some good, for the ads indicate that people are trying to resume their usual life, with usual purchases and amusements. Suits and dresses continue getting cheaper, so more are being sold. Underwear's also getting cheaper and in the underwear market the manufacturers have brought about a revolution. For women brassieres are in; for men BVDs are out, having been replaced by shorts and sleeveless shirts for every man but Mencken. Food, though, is edging up; leg of lamb is now advertised at 35¢ a pound against 20¢ in 1932. Liquor is being advertised and its makers are plainly prospering. Prosperity has its perils, however. The Associated Brewers of Maryland have purchased a full page to warn us that in Annapolis a senate bill proposes a beer tax of $1 a barrel. The brewers predict in sepulchral tones, "If this bill is passed the 5¢ glass of beer is doomed."

Somehow Marylanders survive that threat. Greater problems lie ahead: six more years of depression and then the advent of World War II.

Vignette: The Home Front

The nation organized itself in a far-reaching effort to defeat Germany and Japan. It was a rare Marylander who didn't feel the shock waves of World War II. The draft and the boom in war industries especially in the Baltimore area were the major reasons. As the war went along, the draft widened inexorably. The first draftees were eighteen-year-olds, single and full of vim, but the last ones were thirty-eight-year olds, apt to be family men, settled and spavined. The industrial boom was enormous. As early as September 1942, Mencken wrote a friend, "The town is completely surrounded by plants engaged in war work." By the end of the first year of the war the shipyards of Bethlehem-Fairfield and Maryland Drydock had contracts so huge that they needed 12,000 more employees—and this in a state where because of the depression new jobs had been nearly nonexistent. And the Martin Company had orders for $743,000,000 in aircraft and the need to add 6,000 employees to the 23,000 it already had. They thronged in, not only from Baltimore and the rest of Maryland but from Appalachia and the South, lured by war wages. Among them were many women. Rosie the Riveter had arrived in Baltimore.

The war transformed the fabric of everyday life for old Baltimoreans and new. Men and women craved guidance in coping with the extensive changes that confronted them and so, not infrequently, they wrote to their newspapers. Faced by a flood of inquiries, the *Evening Sun,* with a stroke of genius, drafted Richard Hart of the Enoch Pratt Library to conduct a column on "Your Wartime Problems." He proved to be a sensible and humane counselor. Each day he answered a query of general interest in some detail and than added less-detailed answers to two or three minor queries. There were more questions about the impact of the draft on the family—mainly how to deal with a husband's induction into the army—than on anything else. But the variety was wide.

Among Hart's columns for the first half of 1943 there's one, for example, in which he answers D. B. McK.'s query about preparing for military life. He's an office worker, aged thirty-two, heavy and sedentary, who's gotten his draft notice. Hart's advice is the opposite of high-flown. He says, start getting your feet in shape; walk where you used to ride. Another is on how to treat a soldier husband when he's come home on leave. "Let him flick ashes on the rug"; "keep some beer in the refrigerator for him and cook him man-sized meals. Don't crowd his nights with parties for your relatives; make even his objectionable cronies welcome on his leave." Another column advises soldiers' wives to find a job, preferably in a defense plant but, failing that, any job even if it's only a part-time one in a doctor's office. Another answers a question about how to address members of the armed forces. Hart starts with generals (you call them "General") and goes down through the ranks. Still another column stems from a wife's confession that she shouldn't have written a waspish letter to her husband's commanding officer, for her husband has now missed a promotion to corporal. Right; don't write, is Hart's response.

Then there are the brief answers, for the same period, to the questions of more limited interest. For example, the reply to Helen J. telling her she doesn't have a chance in the world of joining her husband in North Africa even though he's an officer. Or the one to Emma J. P. telling her that the easiest way to get her husband out of the army is through a letter from his old employer attesting that there's a defense job waiting for him back at the shipyard. Or the one to Mrs. D. H. B. and others telling them that it's impossible—simply impossible—for Hart to help them personally to fill out their income tax forms. Or the one to Private W. E. H. telling him that he shouldn't announce to his nurse, who's after all a superior officer, that he's fallen hopelessly in love with her.

Although Hart wrote these particular columns midway in the war, they were probably the more helpful because he took a long view. He knew the war would end sooner or later and he reminded his readers. The postwar world was waiting.

22. Hail Columbia

Nothing is ever first. In America, before Columbia, Greenbelt was created. And before Greenbelt, Radburn and Sunnyside, and—over in England—Welwyn Garden City. So precedents for planning existed, though they were pitifully few. Too often the cities of America were a chaos of uncoordinated growth. The basic question in doing anything from laying out a suburban development to slapping together a shanty was: will it pay?

Then came the New Deal and its projects. President Roosevelt conjured up the Resettlement Administration in September 1935, naming a member of his "Brain Trust," ebullient Rexford Guy Tugwell, to head it. It swiftly became one of the most openhanded of New Deal agencies. Gurney Breckenfeld has noted in his book *Columbia and the New Cities* that it spent $450 million in just two years. Much of the money went into frantic efforts to move people from poor localities to better ones. But some went into the planning and building of three New Towns, made up of rental housing, among which Greenbelt became best known.

The planners laid it out on portions of a tract of 3,370 acres in Prince Georges County about thirteen miles from midtown Washington. The tract was second-growth woodland and farmland ruined by too many crops of tobacco. The construction was uneven since Tugwell insisted on using largely unskilled laborers, who were part of the biggest pool of unemployed. The plan itself wasn't impaired, though, and the building specifications were good. The plan provided for superblocks mainly of row houses, all of which faced not a street but a grassy common. Auto traffic was shunted outside the blocks; within them were pedestrian walkways. A housewife could wheel her baby carriage to the stores at the town center without ever crossing a street; when she came to one there was an underpass. The building specifications called for cinder-block walls, so that the neighbors couldn't be heard; metal-framed casement windows; and metal kitchen cabinets.

When Greenbelt opened in 1937, its first residents were picked by a special committee. There were two requirements: they had to be low-income, earning between $1,000 and $1,200 a year; and they had to reflect the nation's current mixture of religious preferences, 63 percent Protestant, 30 percent Catholic, and 7 percent Jewish.

Greenbelt soon acquired the reputation of being a pleasant, stimulating place to live. An atmosphere developed of social and political awareness. In line with New Deal thinking, the little businesses at the town center were co-operatives. About running them the townspeople debated endlessly, regardless of the importance of the issue. They were perfectly willing to argue about how much a haircut should cost at the Greenbelt barbershop. At any election time the turnout of voters was higher than in other Prince Georges municipalities.

However, trouble was waiting for Greenbelt and her two sister cities. It lay in the fact that they were daring experiments contrary to American custom. The New Deal uneasily shifted control of its New Towns from one federal agency to another. Congress was never really sympathetic to the planning the towns represented; consequently, after the war, in 1949, it voted to sell them to private investors, beginning with the renters already living in them. The residents of Greenbelt formed a housing co-operative, secured a large loan from Nationwide Insurance Company, and took over control of the town. Lacking the money to carry out any new projects in harmony with the old ones, they sold off land they couldn't develop. Though the town sank slowly toward the average, it kept much of its character and continued to maintain many of its urban amenities. Rex Tugwell himself moved there.

With the advent of the 1950s the nation experienced a phenomenal building boom, especially in housing. Maryland shared in it and nowhere more than in Prince Georges. There its so-called developers threw together acre after acre of bulky red-brick boxes and termed them garden apartments. They bought other acres, split them into minimum lots, and squeezed minimum houses onto them. Many acres were wooded to begin with. These the developers bulldozed down to the red clay underneath because it was cheaper to build without the bother of trees. Afterward they set out a few seedlings and called it landscaping. It was as if Greenbelt had never existed.

From his vantage point in Baltimore a far different developer watched the process, particularly in Prince Georges and Baltimore itself, with dismay. He was an Eastern Shoreman named James Rouse, born in 1914 and raised in secluded Easton. The neighborly, placid life he knew there looked all the better to him after he moved to the city. He spent the years 1934–1936 as a legal clerk in the Baltimore office of the Federal Housing Administration and then decided to become a mortgage banker. Although his career was interrupted by naval service in World War II, it was impressive from the outset. He was soon marked as both a shrewd and a civic-minded businessman. His *Who's Who* entries listed some of the organizations he helped to lead during the 1950s and afterward, among them the Greater Baltimore Committee, the United World Federalists of Maryland, the American Council to Improve Our Neighborhoods (ACTION), and the Business Committee for the Arts.

He expanded from mortgage banking into building, with shopping centers becoming his most impressive creation. Breckenfeld has quoted Rouse as remarking, "It was really shopping centers that brought us into the new town business." [1] In the early 1960s he built the village of Cross Keys in northwest Baltimore not far from the city limits. It mixed town houses, garden apartments, high-rise apartments, a village square with stores around it, and an office building complex; and it interspersed them with handsome lawns and trees. It was a stride toward Rouse's ideal: a planned community designed to enhance the lives of the people in it and to earn a profit at the same time.

To attain that ideal he drew extensively on current sociology and economics, utilizing experts whenever he could. What they

1. Gurney Breckenfeld, *Columbia and the New Cities* (New York: Ives Washburn, 1971), p. 222.

didn't know he proposed to have them find out. He settled on Howard County as the best site for his own New Town. Attractive and still rural, the county lay between Baltimore and Washington. Buying piece by piece he acquired what became the site of Columbia. The buying had to be done cloak-and-dagger fashion, in conspiratorial secrecy, for a simple reason: if landowners had discovered what he was up to, they would have raised their prices to the sky. By the time he was through he owned a tenth of the county, twenty-two square miles.

Despite Rouse's caution, money was a major problem. He borrowed it, mainly from the Connecticut General Life Insurance Company, and knew that if he didn't move expeditiously the interest alone on what was ultimately $50 million would abort the project. On the first $23 million it amounted to about $5,000 a day. In October 1963 he confronted the Howard County Commissioners with the disconcerting fact that a substantial slice of their county now belonged to him—and that he proposed to erect a city on it. Would they let him? Their impulse was to give him a resounding no, the more so since it would certainly be the impulse of their constitutents as well. But wisely they said maybe. Then and later he worked with the wiles of a Balkan diplomat to persuade the commissioners and their constituents that the alternative to his planned growth was not a permanently rural county but a spreading fungus of uncoordinated growth like that Prince Georges was experiencing.

For many months he played the role of evangelist. He crisscrossed the county talking with any groups willing to listen, from, as Breckenfeld notes, grand jurors to volunteer firemen. A bald, round-faced man who dressed in tweed jackets and wore loafers, he looked average and trustworthy. He needed to. Not the least obstacle was the covert fear of whites that Columbia would draw many of Baltimore's poor blacks. Rouse announced firmly that Columbia would be integrated. With an engaging mixture of candor and guile he gradually gained popular support. Two years after his meeting with the commissioners, opinion polls showed that at least two-thirds of the people in the county endorsed Rouse's idea.

At the same time that he was evangelizing he was augmenting

his staff and consulting additional experts in order to make the plans for Columbia increasingly specific. For example: if he was right, as an enemy of size, that living in a village was more humane than living in a city, could a city be made up of villages; and, if so, how big could the villages and the city be?

In August 1965 he won. The commissioners consented and the county passed a "New Town District" zoning ordinance which awarded him the free hand with zoning he had to have. A year later construction began on the first village, named Wilde Lake after the ex-chairman of Connecticut General, Frazar Wilde. A year after that the Warren Smith family of San Antonio, having bought a two-storey colonial, were the first householders to move in. Columbia was on its way.

The development during the next decade was phenomenal, even though slowed by the time of the early 1970s because of the recession which set in throughout the United States. Rouse and his associates designed Columbia as a city of, ultimately, more than 100,000 people. But it was a sizable city with a difference and the difference was built in. To achieve the neighborliness and sense of community Rouse hoped for, the city was envisioned as a cluster of villages, each containing from 10,000 to 15,000 persons, and within each village three neighborhoods with between 3,500 and 4,000 persons. And that was the way it developed. Each village had at its core a collection of shops, with either a junior high school ("middle school") or a senior high school or both. Each neighborhood had an elementary school as its center, along with playgrounds, parks, a swimming pool, and a community meeting place. The only shop was a "convenience store."

The broad acres of Columbia began to fill under the farseeing gaze of Rouse's staff. For Columbia, his people and Connecticut General's were now combined as the Howard Research and Development Corporation, "HRD" for short, but the animating spirit remained Rouse's. No plan was too grand, no detail too small for HRD to deal with. It even put a young woman in charge of place names. She chose the names of the villages mainly from Howard County's past. But because she liked literature she often went to authors for others. Where but in Columbia would we find "Faulkner Ridge," named after William Faulkner, with the names of its streets, courts, and cúl-de-sacs drawn from his books? At times the names she gave sounded cute, Hobbits Glen or Scarecrow Court, for example, but few residents objected. By the end of the city's first ten years the named and activated villages besides Wilde Lake were Harpers Choice, Oakland Mills, Long Reach, Owen Brown, Hickory Ridge, and Kings Contrivance.

Rouse hadn't wanted a dormitory suburb but a balanced, viable city. So plans for business and industry were devised from the outset. At the end of ten years some 20,000 persons, many of them townspeople, had jobs in Columbia. If they couldn't walk to work, at least they didn't face the daily grind of commuting a score of miles. About 700 businesses were operating by then. Downtown, around a major mall, office buildings went up, attracting such well-known tenants as A. & P., Shell Oil, Hershey Foods, and—appropriately—Connecticut General. The mall grew to include more than a hundred stores; each village center contained about twenty and these were often operated by local people—neighbors serving neighbors.

At the edges of the city HRD provided industrial parks. The most spectacular was the General Electric Appliance Park East; its coming to Columbia was a coup for Rouse. G. E. invested some $250 million in its plant, the largest investment of the sort in Maryland's history. The other parks established were Guilford, Sieling, and Oakland Ridge. No heavy industry was allowed: no auto body works, for instance, no boiler factories.

The 43,000 people who followed the Warren Smiths to Columbia during its initial decade turned out to be exceptional in a number of ways. They included few older couples and few singles of any age. Columbia became a city of families, with the average family having three to four persons in it. Whether Columbia's jobholders worked in its offices, shops, or industrial parks—or outside of Columbia—the median income of their households was almost $26,000 a year. Of the household heads, 90 percent had gone to college and 42 percent had done graduate work. The chances were that their children could do still better. The neighborhood primary schools, the four middle schools, and the two high schools were all part of an innovative school system. Further education, both vocational and liberal arts, could come from the Howard Community College; and beyond its two-year program there were the university classes organized in Columbia by Antioch, Johns Hopkins, and Loyola of Baltimore.

To offer some of the amenities of life Rouse established the Columbia Association, soon known simply as "CA," financed by an annual fee of 75 cents per $100 of assessed valuation of all taxable property. Once it was in its stride it provided everything for Columbians from a bus line to an ice rink, from boating to karate. With its support the Columbia Athletic Club offered standard sports fare to both men and women. A dozen neighborhood pools supplemented the elaborate swim center. The visual arts center offered instruction in arts and handicrafts including ceramics. The nursery schools and day-care centers eased the load for working mothers—and fathers. Special-interest clubs sprang up, with encouragement from CA, plus a miscellany of other associations. And for children and adults CA maintained the 1,900 acres of parks, playgrounds, and open space that the Rouse plan provided.

For Columbia's culture the capstone was the Merriweather Post Pavilion. Named for a Washington philanthropist but paid for by HRD, it was designed for audiences both within and without the pavilion. Its sides and back opened on grassy slopes where listeners could lounge at a nominal cost. It was at the pavilion that the Baltimore Symphony and the National Symphony played and other musical groups and star performers could be heard.

Columbia's first five years were a honeymoon. Rouse's talent for envisioning the city's future and providing for it humanely was astonishing. On the other hand he was no prophet and he failed to foresee the recession. It hurt Columbia, changed its nature somewhat, and stunted its growth. Another emerging problem, with many aspects, was not only economic but psychological: the residents' high expectations. HRD advertised Columbia as the "Next America" and then fell victim to its advertising. Columbia couldn't become Utopia. Moving there couldn't make everyone different and better. Distraught couples found that Columbia couldn't heal a festering marriage though they thought it should. Columbia couldn't make its builders, who bought land from Rouse, build carefully in a period of careless building; new roofs leaked in Columbia as they did everywhere else. Columbia couldn't resolve a variety of other problems to universal satisfaction, among them those involving integration, crime control, cultural affairs, and self-government. But it tried to and more often than not did fairly well.

Here the newspapers of the 1970s reflect, as they frequently do, the problems more clearly than the solutions. However, among the major papers the *Baltimore Sun* reported on both as well as any. On June 13, 1974, it ran a representative story on Rouse's efforts to cope with the recession. It was on his petitioning for a zoning change to allow him to build 4,342 more apartments, town houses, and condominium units and 3,680 fewer single-family detached homes. His main argument was that the market for such homes had dropped drastically because the interest rates on mortgages had nearly doubled. His figures supported his plea. The *Sun* for July 27, 1974, noted that house sales and rentals had sunk 20 percent in the course of the recession up to that time. After more than two years of negotiating, the Howard County Zoning Board consented to the change. Agreement came partly because the county council now had four Columbians among its five members and the Columbians saw Rouse's point, as did the new county executive, Dr. Edward Cochran, a progressive physicist from a town near Columbia. Rouse could now embark on his altered course.

Integration posed another problem. Reporter Matthew Seiden analyzed it in the *Sun* for October 22, 1972. Though the proportion of blacks by the early 1970s was nearing 20 percent, they were largely members of the black bourgeoisie. The middle-class whites and the middle-class blacks lived together amicably enough. Seiden checked a lane in Bryant Woods, for instance, with four white and three black families living on it and found that "without exception, these people say that they get along fine together." But poor blacks were rarely moving in and when they did tensions were apt to appear. Columbia was able to provide only a minimum of subsidized housing. Rouse had hoped for 10 percent; he was getting 3 percent. Only 1,000 units out of 20,000 in Columbia were available to low- or moderate-income families of either race. So there was a racial but not an economic mix. Among the teen-agers there was apparently neither. Seiden's impression was that the black teen-agers were truculent and the white ones standoffish.

Then there was crime. Under the revealing headline "Columbia did not Anticipate Rise in Crime," the *Sun* for October 7, 1972, reported the latest incident. Three young toughs had forced their way into a town house on Harpers Road, had kicked one man in the jaw, had shot another, and had left with $150 and several pieces of stereo equipment. Howard County's police department said defensively that almost half the county's crime, mainly muggings and burglaries, was taking place within Columbia. Some of the old-timers in the county were reported as charging that Columbia criminals were Columbia-bred; the city's general manager, Michael Spear, replied evasively that "Columbia is the victim more than the perpetrator of crime."

Cultural affairs presented a different kind of difficulty. Rouse's original plan called for a high degree of involvement by Columbians but it didn't work out that way. The arts, especially, were in trouble by the start of the 1970s. Washington's Corcoran School of Art stopped supporting its Columbia branch in early 1970. The Peabody Institute canceled its music classes in June 1971. Antioch College, which had opened its Columbia branch with much fanfare, quietly scaled down its activities. The Post Pavilion started in the red and stayed there. Its only profits came from the rock concerts, which were plagued with unruly audiences of outsiders. The visual arts center was reported by 1975 as being "hard-pressed." On the other hand, Howard Community College expanded every year. Many other cultural and educational activities continued although on a modest scale.

Self-government, or rather the lack of it, was another sore spot. The typical Columbian was not only better-educated but more aggressive politically, it seemed, than the average Marylander. Rouse had provided meeting space both in the villages and in the neighborhoods for the citizens. Naturally meetings were held, officers chosen, actions taken. By early 1977 some of the village board members and other community leaders were pressing harder than ever for control over CA, with the evident next step being control over the whole city. Some of the resentment against Rouse was understandable. He personified the forces in HRD which had postponed "independence" from 1977 to 1985. The damaging effect of the recession was a salient reason but by no means a persuasive one to the ambitious community leaders.

Their prospects of victory were good. In April 1977 Columbia residents elected a town council unanimously committed to self-government. The American tradition of autonomy kept its force and time was on their side. But this election did not mean that Columbians had been or were now discontented with Columbia.

Michael Clark started his *Sun* story of September 24, 1973, with: "A survey of 1000 Columbia families shows widespread resident satisfaction with life in the new city and increased contacts between persons of different races and social backgrounds." The *Sun* of October 2, 1976, summarized a survey commissioned by the National Science Foundation. The highlight of the survey was that 80 percent of the residents stood ready to recommend Columbia to their friends "as a good place to move to." The neighborliness Rouse always hoped for had developed, in the city, in the villages, in the neighborhoods. And even within the neighborhoods, for Rouse with a typical touch had decreed that the mailboxes be clustered together every 200 feet so that householders half a dozen doors apart would have occasion to greet one another.

The first time that the journalist Lincoln Steffens traveled to Soviet Russia he came back with stars in his eyes. "I have seen the future," he proclaimed, "and it works." Without prejudice we might say that about Columbia also.

The new and the old: as Maryland advanced toward the future it nicely illustrated both. While Columbia, the city which carried planning further than it had ever been carried in

America, was adding new residents every year, many other cities in the state were losing to the countryside. This was an astonishing reversal of a decades-old trend, which as early as 1910 had reached the point where more Marylanders were living in the cities than on the farms.

The census estimates for 1975 revealed a rise in the state's population of 4.4 percent since 1970. During that period the city of Baltimore, instead of gaining, lost 6 percent. Of the two dormitory suburbs around Washington, Prince Georges and Montgomery counties, the first lost population and the second slowed its growth to a crawl. On the other hand, the Eastern Shore and western Maryland got more than their anticipated share of newcomers, as Lawrence Feinberg reported in an article in the *Washington Post* for July 6, 1976. Five of the eight Eastern Shore counties lost population during the 1960s but in the 1970s they began to gain. Caroline showed the sharpest reversal, from a 4 percent loss in the 1960s to an 8.6 percent gain in the first half of the 1970s. Even Somerset, least prosperous of counties, gained 2.8 percent after losing people for close to a century. In western Maryland, rugged Garrett County exemplified the shift, though less strikingly than the Eastern Shore counties. During the 1960s it gained 5.2 percent, during the first half of the 1970s, 8.9 percent.

Today most Americans probably concede that change isn't necessarily progress. Yet it's interesting to see a tilt toward the past taking place. Naturally we'll never return to the agrarian Maryland of Daniel Dulany. That was almost another country. Yet it's heartening to some of us to see rural life recovering part of its importance and to find the recovery greater than anyone expected. The lesson perhaps is that no one can foretell Maryland's future. All we can do is hope that it will be good.

Suggestions for Further Reading

These suggestions are intended for the general reader. They name works providing an introduction to Maryland's past and an explanation of some parts of Maryland's present.

We can begin with Donald Dozer's painstaking *Portrait of the Free State: A History of Maryland* (Cambridge, Md.: Tidewater Publishers, 1976). Our most comprehensive account is *Maryland: A History 1632–1974* (Baltimore: Maryland Historical Society, 1974). Ably edited by Richard Walsh and William Lloyd Fox, it contains ten substantial chapters, each by a different specialist. The book offers us social history in its broadest sense, often drawing on recent advances in research in the social sciences. At the opposite extreme and not without charm is Matthew Page Andrews's *History of Maryland: Province and State* (Garden City, N.Y.: Doubleday, Doran, 1929; facsimile reprint, Hatboro, Pa.: Tradition Press, 1965). As Andrews announced in his preface, "Stress is laid upon colonial origins." The tone of the book is patriotic and conservative. Behind Andrews's book loom the heavy volumes by J. Thomas Scharf. In his histories of Baltimore, western Maryland, and Maryland as a whole, we see old-style local history abundantly detailed. They are better for browsing than concentrated reading.

On early Maryland we can read Aubrey Land's excellent *The Dulanys of Maryland* (Baltimore: Maryland Historical Society, 1955; republication, Baltimore: Johns Hopkins University Press, 1968). It relates the lives of Daniel Dulany the Elder and Daniel Dulany the Younger to the whole sweep of the eighteenth century in Maryland. Charles Barker's *The Background of the Revolution in Maryland* (New Haven: Yale University Press, 1940; reprint, Hamden, Conn.: Shoe String Press, 1967) also amply repays our reading.

Among a diversity of other books, mainly recent, which a reader might like are: William Warner's *Beautiful Swimmers: Watermen, Crabs, and the Chesapeake Bay* (Boston: Little, Brown, 1976); Boyd Gibbons's *Wye Island* (Baltimore: Johns Hopkins University

199

Press, 1977); Hulbert Footner's *Maryland Main and the Eastern Shore* (New York: D. Appleton-Century, 1942; reprint, Hatboro, Pa.: Tradition Press, 1967); Katherine Harvey's *The Best-Dressed Miners: Life and Labor in the Maryland Coal Region 1835–1910* (Ithaca: Cornell University Press, 1969); Alexandra Lee Levin's *The Szolds of Lombard Street: A Baltimore Family, 1859–1909* (Philadelphia: Jewish Publication Society of America, 1960); and Francis Beirne's *The Amiable Baltimoreans* (New York: Dutton, 1951) and *Baltimore: A Picture History, 1858–1958* (New York: Hastings House, 1957). More illuminating than many another volume is Maryland's *Historical Atlas: A Review of Events and Forces that have Influenced the Development of the State* ([n. p.] 1973), a co-operative effort involving the state's department of economic and community development, the state's department of planning, and the Washington firm of Raymond, Parish, Pine & Plavnick.

Lastly, there's no better nourishment for a continuing interest in our state's history than the *Maryland Historical Magazine,* published quarterly by the Maryland Historical Society.

Index

201